FISHING GOWER

A guide to shore fishing
the Gower Peninsula

By
Malcolm Halfpenny

2006

ISBN 0 948891 04 1

Printed by Dinefwr Press
Rawlings Road, Llandybie
Carmarthenshire
SA18 3YD

With thanks to
my wife Patricia for her perseverance.

and family
Stephen, Michael, Estelle
Rhian, Leigh and Rachel

Contents

Venues

Introduction

Buy the Ordnance Survey Map Pathfinder 1126 of the Gower, $2^1/_2$ inches to 1 mile, map scale 1:25,000, available in most bookshops.

The map is divided into a number of squares with national grid numbers alongside.

To use these national grid numbers *(NGR)* read the numbers along the bottom first, and then the numbers upwards and where the lines intersect is the *NGR* number.

e.g. to find SKYSEA in PORT
EYNON BAY
NGR 474/844

A guide to distance on the map – each square is divided into ten sections and each section is 4 millimetres, which is a distance of 100 metres, map scale 1:25,000

Map scale 1:50,000
100 metres equals 2 millimetres on the map.

It is also important to buy a SWANSEA BAY Tide table, for the tide information in this book.

Foreword

This small fishing book is intended to help the newcomer/holiday maker to the Peninsula, and hopefully be of some help to the local fisherman/woman as to where and how to fish, with directions.

There are about one hundred and sixty different kinds of fish that are reasonably common around the British Isles, but our species around Gower are mainly – Cod on the Swansea breakwater; Garfish at Pennard; Bream at Oxwich Point; Bass and Mullet at Llangennith; Flounder along the estuaries, through to the occasional Tope at the Lynch sand channel at Broughton.

The more popular holiday beaches like Langland, Caswell, Oxwich and Port Eynon etc., will be crowded during the Summer months, so search out the more secluded bays like Falls, Tears Point, Whitford and the rock marks.

Just a word of caution, there are a number of areas at which to be extra careful whilst fishing the Gower Peninsula, especially the marsh areas along the Burry estuary, all the way up the River Loughor to Llangennech. So until you familiarise yourself with the area, only fish the marshes on a low tide – 10.6 metres on the Swansea tide table. Finally, watch the tides on the three cut-off islands, Worms Head, Burry Holmes and the Middle and Outer Head at Mumbles.

David Bateman Ltd. www.bateman.co.nz

Swansea Breakwater and East Pier

Bait	Black Lug & Crab

Fishing off the Swansea Breakwater Walls, one of the more popular winter venues for Cod and Whiting. The sea wall is numbered from number 79 to 1.

The sandier areas are from 79 down to 24, then it becomes more rocky to number 1. The access points over the wall are at numbers 52, 40 & 23.

A clipped down single hook rig is advised with black lug, casting as far as possible. High tides seem to be most productive. Try all the more popular baits for Cod. Black and Blow lug, Squid and Mackerel.

Black lug can be pumped Eastwards towards the two cooling towers at Llandarcy oil refinery at bottom water. Soft and peeler crab amongst the stones, also towards the East Pier just before bottom water, preferably on Spring Tides.

Venue 1 – Fishing the East Pier, walk out on the top catwalk and try fishing, midway above an old wreck, to your left Eastwards.

Venue 2 – Continue to the end and fish above the half round handrail platform, casting out towards the INNER FAIRWAY BUOY.

Venue 3 – The seaward side of the wall at number 1, is known as Cod Corner, with not quite so many rocks.

Rocky venues – use rotten bottom rigs.

Swansea East Pier

Directions

Coming out of Swansea, take the A483 to Cardiff Road and watch for the 4 Counties warehouse on your right, turn left opposite, by the large advertising board, you will see Gower Chemicals in front of you. (If you miss this turning carry on to the roundabout and come back down Fabian Way). Turn right at Blazers Caravans, under the road bridge up to a keep left sign.

Turn left at the sign Swansea dry docks/Stores jetty, drive along this road with the sea wall on your left, and oil tanks on your right.

Coming from the Cardiff area across the New Briton Ferry road bridge, take the Swansea turn off (junction 42) and travel along Fabian Way, turn left at the sign Queens Dock and Oil terminals, to meet up with the road from Swansea.

The sea wall has numbers along its entire length from 79 down to 1. Follow the road along and turn left at number 7 and drive to a small parking area by number 1, to fish the East Pier.

An Association British Ports License is required to fish the East and West Piers and also the Breakwater, obtainable from:

Association of British Ports, Harbour Office, Lockhead, Kings Dock, Swansea SA1 1QR. Telephone: 01792 33221.

Application form to fill in *(copy of which is at the rear of the book).* Fee (2005) is £26.50 (£5.30 O.A.P.)

Small Harbour just at the start of East Pier

Swansea Marina and West Pier

Bait	No

The West pier is a very popular summer venue for Mackerel. Walk along the pier to about the midway mark on the bend to fish for Mackerel, casting over the wall westwards into Swansea Bay and fishing out on the end of the pier in winter months for Cod and Whiting.

Try fishing the Marina for Mullet with very light tackle and size 4 or 6 hooks with harbour ragworm.

At the car park by the River Barrage is the Swansea Sea Angling Centre & Rogers Tackle, which is open 7 days a week. Telephone number 01792 469999. Bookings are taken here for boat trips.

There are a couple of tugs working out of Swansea docks called 'Caswell' and 'Langland'.

Swansea foreshore with Council offices in the background

Directions

Travelling from the Cardiff area along the M4 across the new Briton Ferry road bridge, take the Swansea turn off, junction 42 and travel down Fabian Way into Swansea on the A4067. Follow the sign for Gower and Marina, past the Swansea Leisure Centre, and turn left at the traffic lights in front of the County Hall down BATHHURST Street to the end and park in the small car park at the River Barrage sign.

Alternatively from the Carmarthen areas, come off the M4 at Junction 47, and follow the sign to Swansea on the A483 down to the round-about, turn right onto A484 to Llanelli, then left at the sign Gowerton B4296, travel under the railway bridge, straight through at the first set of lights. Turn left at the next set of traffic lights, after 100 yards or so take the right hand fork B4296 Dunvant/Killay. At Killay follow the sign for Sketty A4118, set mileometer to zero here and after 1.4 miles turn right at the sign for Singleton Hospital and Mumbles (3 miles), drive down through a set of traffic lights to a mini roundabout, turn left at the sign Mumbles (3 miles). Through two sets of traffic lights past Singleton Hospital on the left, and at the T-junction turn left on the A4067 to Swansea City Centre. Travel past Swansea University and Swansea R.F.C. ground, then get in the outside lane at this point and drive under the footbridge past County Hall, turn right at the second set of traffic lights by the red brick houses and the Marriot Hotel.

The Marina with sea angling boats in the foreground

County Hall/Blackpill to West Cross

Blackpill NGR619/907

Bait	Blow Lug

The area known as Blackpill is not over fished because one of the reasons is that the sandy bay is so flat it gives a limited amount of time with any depth of water around the high water mark, so it gives the impression of not being very productive. But one of the favoured Cod locations during the winter is near the swigg buoy, in front of County Hall. There is a small boating lake/paddling pool and playground nearby, with the river Clyne running into the sea, a popular holiday location during the summer months.

West Cross *NGR 614/895*

The same type of fishing as Blackpill, $1\frac{1}{2}$ hours either side of high water, but you can dig some lug here and fish the tide in.

Fish two rods, one with baited spoon, the other with running ledger. Fishing for Flounder and School Bass. There is sand along the entire length from County Hall to West Cross, and is a popular blow lug diggers beach. Both venues are fished best on spring tides.

Blackpill and West Cross are difficult venues to fish because the beach is so flat, therefore the tide goes out a long way.

Roman Bridge at Blackpill, Clyne stream beneath

Directions

Fishing the Swansea Bay area from the County Hall to West Cross is a relatively flat beach with some access and parking along its length. But I have picked out just two venues, Blackpill and West Cross.

To fish the area at the Lido Boating and Paddling Pool at Blackpill, travel out of Swansea towards Mumbles along the A4067 past Backpill Burrows public golf course (9 holes) and when you pass the Shell Garage on your right get into the outside lane, and take the second turning on the right at the sign 'The BOMBAY SPICE' restaurant opposite the small boating lake. Park the car opposite the restaurant and walk back across the busy main road to the beach.

For West Cross carry on past the Lido Boating lake straight on through a set of traffic lights to a mini roundabout, turn right at a sign for West Cross, then first left and first left again down past a small shopping precinct and park-in a small car park at the end of the road. Free parking. Cross the road at the Pelican traffic lights down alongside the West Cross public house to the foreshore.

The small boating/paddling lake at Blackpill – *now redesigned*

Knab Rock

NGR 628/876

Bait	Blow Lug

Fishing the Knab is off the sea wall with rods propped on the hand rails, some two hours either side of top water onto sand.

Popular venue winter months where the occasional big Cod can be caught. Try this venue during the hours of darkness under the Globe type lights. Distance casting is not really necessary owing to the small boats anchored close to the wall.

My favoured area is at the right hand side at the second last set of Globe lights by the last seat nearest to Knab Rock. This area is a little more clear of anchored and moored boats, where if you fancy a long cast, try here.

Most popular baits, blow lug, but also try black lug if you can get it, also squid and fish baits.

End rigs will vary depending on distance and bait.

Can be very windswept in winter, so take plenty of warm food and clothing, but the car is quite near to hand for shelter.

Mumbles foreshore, from 'Knab Rock' to Mumbles Pier

Directions

Follow the A4067 from Swansea to Mumbles past Blackpill Burrows golf course. Drive through Blackpill straight on at the mini roundabout, past West Cross Hotel on your left to the mini roundabout at Oystermouth, with the White Rose Public House facing you. Drive straight on and the entrance to fishing the area known as Knab Rock is right opposite Mumbles Yacht Club at Southend.

Knab Rock promenade is a new developed tarmacadam area with two slipways for launching small boats.

There is a parking fee during the summer months but free during the winter.

Old site of Lime Kiln at 'Knab Rock', Mumbles

Mumbles Pier, Middle and Outer Head
Mumbles Outer Head NGR 635/872 (Mumbles Lighthouse built 1794)

Bait	Crab

N.B. One of the cut off islands.

As a rough guide to crossing, you can cross to the outer head on a 38.4 foot/11.7 metre tide 2 hours and 20 minutes before bottom water, with the use of wellingtons, a little longer for the tide to totally recede. Take care if fishing the outer or middle heads or the tide will cut you off. The tide will come in first between the outer sound, and then the inner sound, by the Cinderellas/Pier Hotel night club.

Couple of venues to fish on the outer head, one is beneath the lighthouse in front of 'Bobs' cave into a gully on the extreme end of the rocks, out onto the Mixon Sands, be very careful out here. The other is on the eastern side below the lighthouse, access is by way of steps up over the top, or you can go round both sides by way of the rocks. These are rotten bottom venues, single hook crab for Bass in summer.

Lug/fish/Rag/Crab in Winter

Winter fishing needs plenty of warm food and clothing and if you are unfortunate or decide to fish the tide in and out, and be cut off, and the weather turns inclement, there are a couple of shelters. One is half way up the steps on the right, the other also on the eastern side at the top, a lookout post beneath the lighthouse. *NGR 635/872*

Mumbles Pier

Directions

Travelling through Swansea to Mumbles on the A4067 past Blackpill Burrows golf course, follow the road all the way past Oystermouth, past a small playground and village lane slipway. The access road to Mumbles Pier is on the left hand side just after you pass Mumbles Yacht Club, park the car near the Amusement Arcade.

Mumbles Pier *NGR 633/875*

The Pier toll 1999, for a single rod is £3.00 Best fishing is out on the end, but you will need to get there early on a Saturday and Sunday during the Cod season. If the end is full then fish on the right hand side opposite the catwalk to Mumbles lifeboat station, casting towards Middle Head.

Cod is the main quarry, but a wide variety of species can be caught throughout the year, and a mixture of crab and lug cocktail can be deadly at the right time. (Freeze some crab late in the summer for use during the winter months).

If you start to lose too much tackle, switch to a single hook rotten bottom rig.

There is a 'No Fishing Ban' between Knab Rock and the Amusement Arcade along a private road.

Soft and Peeler Crab can be found amongst the rocks, but as this is a popular holiday resort there are a lot of fishermen searching them out.

Pier opening times *(Open all Year)*:
Early Summer: 9a.m. – 8p.m.
Summer: 9a.m. – 10p.m.
Winter: 9a.m. – 5p.m.

Mumbles Lighthouse
Initially the light was by two coal fires, one above the other in the stone tower. The height of the tower from sea level at Bobs Cave is 114 feet, the range of the light is 19 miles.

Mumbles Pier Inner Sound Beach
NGR 632/873

Bait	Crab

Just below Cinderellas night club is Inner Sound Sandy beach with rocks between the causeway, and on the right hand side you will see a rocky outcrop. Climb up onto these rocks, and fish with single hook crab bait for Bass, when the tide is making through the causeway to Inner Head.

Use a rotten bottom, rig holding the rod at all times. Also try the left side after you descend down the steps, off the rocks casting out into the rocky bay.

Walking out to the lighthouse, which was built in 1794, near middle head, you will cóme across the remains of the railway track, leading out to the wooden winch platform with derelict trams on top, used for the transfer of coal to the lighthouse. Initially the light was by two coal fires one above the other in the stone tower. Later replaced by Argon lamps with reflectors. The lighthouse has a 56 foot high tower, and from 'Bob's' Cave at water level its height is at 114 foot, the light can be seen from a distance of 19 miles.

'Cherry Stones' Bay Middle Island NGR 633/872

Before you cross to the outer Island at bottom water go to the right along the small causeway to 'Cherry Stones' Bay. So called because of the round stones. Fish off the rocks following the tide in, so you are still casting onto clean sand.

The Bass will run through the causeway as the tide makes (Crab bait).

Try this venue in the summer when the beaches are crowded, parking is by the amusement arcade. Also popular shrimping grounds.

You will be cut off by the tide if fishing until top water, but with a little care you can get in a couple of hours fishing before this happens.

Old tramway track out to the Lighthouse

Mumbles Lighthouse above 'Bobs' cave

Bracelet Bay and Tutt Head

Bracelet Bay NGR 630/872

Bait	Small amount of Crab

Bracelet Bay consists of heavy rocks with two stretches of sand on the left hand side. The easiest section to fish is on the eastern side, left with a rotten bottom rig, with a wide variety of species to be caught during the summer months, with whiting and codling during the winter.

Best baits for fishing Bracelet and Tutt are crab in the summer, black and blow lug with fish baits for codling and whiting during the winter.

Tutt Head NGR 628/869 – *Caution required*

It is advisable to check out this venue at bottom water to cut down on tackle losses, but the fishing times for both venues are two hours either side of top water.

Some care is needed during a heavy swell as the waves crash up over the rocks.

I would again suggest a rotten bottom rig, but also try some spinning or live bait fishing in the summer.

This area is known as the Mixon Shoal.

Bracelet Bay

Directions

Driving through Swansea towards Mumbles, on the A4067, past Blackpill Burrows 9 hole golf course on your left, through Blackpill and Oystermouth towards Mumbles pier. Then up the hill after the yacht club through the 'cutting' (which was opened in 1887 for access to Bracelet and Limeslade), then take the first turning left after the green apple into the pay and display car park.

Free parking during the winter months. This car park is suitable for fishing Bracelet Bay, Tutt Head, and also Limeslade.

Park the car on the Eastern side – left, of the bay by the steps if fishing Bracelet and on the Western side – right, by the Admiral Benbow *(as per Treasure Island)* public house if fishing the 'Tutt'.

Access to the rock marks of the Tutt are via a well worn cliff path around the headland beneath the coastguard station.

Tutt Head

Limeslade
NGR 626/869

Bait	Limited Crab

Limeslade is a small rocky cove with a narrow strip of sand in the middle and out in the bay is the Mixon buoy at the entry and guarding the area known as the Mixon Shoal. Worth checking this area at bottom water to save tackle losses.

Clip down rig with black or blow lug for winter codling. Mackerel feathers in summer off the top of the rocks area just before the gate, casting into the bay towards the coastguard station.

Also try on the Westerly side (right) of the Tutt, off the rocks. At bottom water spring tides, there is a stretch of rocks which go well out into the Mixon shoal. Try here casting out over Limeslade Bay looking for the sandy stretch of coast.

Limeslade

24

Directions

Driving through Swansea towards Mumbles on the A4067 past Blackpill Burrows golf course, through Blackpill and Oystermouth towards Mumbles pier, up the hill after the yacht club, through the cutting, then the first turning left after the Green Apple into the Council owned car park. Charges during the summer but free during the winter. Park just off the road below the coastguard station on the right hand side, and walk down to Limeslade Bay.

Some limited parking in the winter months available down by the small cafe and in the summer after 6p.m. Double yellow lines 1st May to 30th September from 9a.m. to 6p.m.

View of rocks back to Bracelet

Rotherslade

Bait	No

If you decide to fish the rocky area between Limeslade and Rotherslade, it needs a survey first at bottom water to search out the gullies, and where at bottom water you can cast onto clean sand.

Midway between Limeslade and Rotherslade as you descend down from 'Rams Tor', around a bend there is a drop into a flat rocky cove, with a fair chance of retrieve at high water. *NGR 617/869*

Whiting/Codling/Mackerel – Tackle losses high

Rotherslade, coming out at the bottom of the shelter onto the sandy beach, you will see in front of you the 'Storrs Rock'. Fish just to the left of this where you will see a patch of rocks out in the bay at bottom water. *NGR 611/872*

The Osbourne Hotel is up behind you built on the crag known as Rotherstor.

A wide variety of species can be taken along this stretch of coastline, Bass/Pollack/to small Ray, so take a mixture of baits and traces for fishing over clean sand.

Rotherslade

Directions

Parking is the same as fishing Limeslade. Walk down past Limeslade Bay up the start of the cliff path, through a gate, follow the cliff path up over 'Rams Tor' and down towards Rotherslade. A distance of about 1½ miles *(see below)*

Access to Rotherslade beach is down steps through a disused concrete shelter, with the Osbourne Hotel above.

Because access to the beach through the shelter* is somewhat of an eyesore, discussions are taking place to upgrade or demolish this structure.

By car to Rotherslade, drive down past Limeslade turn right at a small cafe up Plunch Lane for 1.4 miles (narrow roads) then left at a sign for Osbourne Hotel, and Rotherslade Road is the turning before the sign for Langland. There is very limited parking on the right hand side of the road. Double yellow lines on the left 1st May - 30th September. Walk down the road and access is through the concrete shelter to the beach.

Somewhat easier walk, is to park at Langland and walk back to Rotherslade before the tide is fully in.

* July 1997. Demolition is in progress of the concrete shelter and should be complete by the time of publication.

Storrs Rock

Langland – Snaple Point – Whiteshell Point
NGR 607/874

Bait	Some Crab

Langland beach has a mixture of stone and sand, with some areas of clean sand only.

The easiest section to fish if you have a youngster with you, is directly in front of the St. Johns Ambulance hut and the wooden shelter. So if you arrive at high water, you will be casting onto clean sand at this mark.

The beach attracts a lot of tourists during the summer months and surfers all year, so try Snaple Point.

Snaple Point *NGR 606/868*

Walk around the headland along the path past the golf course, and at Snaple point six yards past the post with the lifebuoy attached is a nice sandy cove to fish. Try a two hook rig here with crab on the bottom, harbour ragworm on the top. Bass and Bream, but a wide variety of fish if the conditions are right.

Whiteshell Point *NGR 598/868*

The area between Snaple Point and Whiteshell Point is far too rocky to fish, but if you are a bit of a fanatic there are one or two small difficult areas past 'Culver Hole' to fish with crab or try float fishing at top water. Worth a check at bottom water. Take bait with you as there is only a limited amount of crab at low water.

Be careful going down the rocks, if fishing here on your own.

Snaple Point

Directions

If I explain directions to this venue, as if travelling from the West Wales areas, these can also be used for fishing around the Mumbles area.

Come off the M4 motorway at junction 47 and follow the sign for Swansea A483, down to a roundabout, turn right to Llanelli A484. Follow this road until you see the sign for Gowerton, turn left on to the B4296, under the railway bridge up the hill and straight on at the traffic lights, at the next set of traffic lights turn left and after 100 yards or so take the right hand fork B4296 for Dunvant/Killay.

When you reach Killay by the big Sketty/Uplands sign A4118, just before the mini roundabout, set the mileometer to zero here. Follow the road towards Sketty and after 1.5 miles turn right at the sign for Singleton Hospital and Mumbles. Down through a set of traffic lights to a mini roundabout, turn left at a sign marked Mumbles 3 miles. Drive down through two sets of traffic lights passing Singleton Hospital, and at the T-junction turn right A4067 towards Mumbles. Drive straight on until you come to a mini roundabout in Oystermouth with the 'White Rose' public house in front of you, turn right for Langland. Up the hill, then turn left at the church signposted Langland and Caswell.

Take the road signposted for Langland Bay down through the traffic lights to a pay and display car park. Free parking winter months.

Langland

Caswell

Bait	No

Caswell Westerly Side *NGR 589/875*

If fishing on the western side of the bay off the large flat concrete platform in front of Freshwater Cave, it is a stony area in front of you for some 20 yards and then clean sand.

You will be cut off here towards high water, but there is a steep climb at the back up over Redley Cliff and then back down to the beach, in front of the Redcliffe apartments.

Very popular surfers beach, summer and winter.

The concrete platform at Freshwater Cave was for fresh water storage, and up above this point on the cliff top, a wooden type windmill was erected sometime in the 1880's to pump water into the village, but fell into disrepair in the early 1930's, and all that remains is an iron rod visible from the beach.

At the entry to the beach opposite the shops, the brick building was another pumping station (half the building has gone) by the slipway ramp. This used to pump water from the Redley spring to the reservoir in Newton.

Caswell Bay

Directions

Drive from Swansea towards Mumbles on the A4067, until you arrive at the mini roundabout at Oystermouth, with the White Rose Public House in front of you, turn right up the hill. Turn left at the Church signposted Langland and Caswell, follow the well signposted signs for Caswell. Park in the pay and display car parks, one on the hill, one at the bottom, free in the winter. Any obstruction by illegal parking will get you a ticket.

Emergency telephone on the beach.

Caswell Easterly Side *NGR 593/874*

Walk around the back of the shops if the tide is in, up the cliff path to fish the rock marks, at the point where you see the post with the emergency buoy attached, casting westwards towards Red Cliff apartments onto clean sand. Or carry on around the headland path to the third post with the emergency buoy attached, scramble down the bank and fish two yards to the left of the post, casting about 25 yards onto shingle. Or fish off the shingle and cast about 20 yards to clear the rocks onto clean sand. Just behind this buoy is a hole in the rocks to stash your gear if fishing in inclement weather.

Another 170 yards around the headland you will come to a large half round type rock with a flatish top (before you reach the seat) in front of which is a shingle and sand gully, use a rotten bottom rig here, or try float fishing off the rock towards high water.

Variety of fish to be caught – some plaice – during the summer months, with crab and harbour rag the most popular.

Whiting and some codling during the winter with Black/Blow lug and Squid.

Brandy Cove *(originally known as Hareslade)*
NGR 586/874

Bait	No

Brandy Cove is a mixture of Rock-shingle and sand, and difficult fishing in front of steps, so fish off 'Cunningham Corner'. Walk about 300 yards to the right around the cliff path, then turn left down a grassy path, and steep descent to a rock mark, casting slightly left, 10 to 15 yards to clear the rocks onto clean sand.

Try this venue for early spring Bass as soon as you can get some crab.

The fishing from Brandy Cove to Pwlldu Bay is a very rugged section of coastline, with a difficult climb down the rocks. One or two possible venues, but expect heavy tackle losses, one is the area known as 'Seven Slades' midway between Brandy Cove and Pwlldu *NGR 582/872*. It would be worth a walk at bottom water to check out.

It is a distance of perhaps $^3/_4$ mile from Brandy Cove to Pwlldu.

From 'Cunningham' corner back to Brandy Cove

Directions

The walk to Brandy Cove from Caswell is something in the region of $\frac{1}{4}$ mile with two main pathways. The easiest is from the car park at Caswell westwards across the beach in front of REDCLIFF apartments, but if the tide is in you will have to go up the hill and descend down the path opposite the Caswell Bay Court. In front of the apartment building, you will see a set of steps at the end which leads up to Redley Cliff path, follow this path around the headland and down some man made steps to Brandy Cove.

Another longer walk to the Cove is from the car park up the hill past Caswell Bay Court, and just after the 30 mph sign turn left at DYFLAN HOUSE down a private road past CRUD-Y-GWYNT (Breeze of the wind) house over a hop up type stile and up the Redley Cliff path to Brandy Cove.

To Brandy Cove from Pyle Corner Bishopston *(see directions PWLLDU page 35)* is just under $\frac{1}{2}$ mile. Take the Brandy Cove road at Pyle corner, park on main road before entry to lane, there is no parking down the lane, walk down the narrow road, then down the lane to Brandy Cove.

Brandy Cove

Pwlldu – Bantam Bay – Graves End

Pwlldu (Blackpool) NGR 575/871

Bait	No

After emerging onto the limestone strewn shoreline, crossing over 'BARLOW' trout stream, which goes under stones and emerges out on the shore. Walk over to the left eastwards onto the rocks, casting from here towards Pwlldu Head onto clean sand, vary your casting distances and try fishing close range.

Fishing in the middle of the Bay, try long range, over limestone onto sand.

Try fishing these two areas either side of top water with two rods, one with single hook crab, the other a paternoster running ledger type rig with worm and fish baits.

On the right hand side of the bay, Westwards, you will see a large boulder at bottom water with a steel ring sunk in the top, Ring Rock. Fish this area with rotten bottom, trying various baits, with only one rod starting about 3 hours before top water.

Bantam Bay *NGR 574/866*

To get to Bantam Bay the easiest access is to traverse the rocks at the back of Ring Rock, arriving at bottom water you will see a stretch of sand running up the bay from left to right. It's best to fish here the first time from bottom water up, for you to get to know how the beach fishes. Use rotten bottom rigs. There is a sheep path up at the back which leads back down to the Bay.

There are a couple of flat rock gullies to fish after Bantam Bay, they are known as Graves End towards Hunts Bay, bottom water venues with crab. But a note of caution, be wary of the tide.

Ring Rock

Directions

Coming through Swansea towards Mumbles on the A4067, passing the public golf course on your left, drive up to the traffic lights, just after the Lido boating lake at Blackpill with a garage on your left. Turn right here, signposted Bishopston/Pennard, follow the road for a couple of miles, drive past the Bishopston Road sign and half way down the hill turn left into Bishopston Road, travel along this road to a sharp left hand bend (Pyle Corner) and turn right at this point into Brandy Cove Road, and sharp right again by the shops into Pwlldu Lane, park along this road.

N.B. There is no parking in the car park at the end known as Pwlldu head car park, it's now blocked off with large boulders. The reason being access required for ambulance and safety services.

After parking, walk down the road about 100 yards and turn left at the private road sign, and follow the road then cliff path to Pwlldu Beach.

The walk from the shops to the two cottages called Beaufort and Ship Cottage on the foreshore is one mile, which will take about 20 to 25 minutes.

Quite a few species can be caught from Pwlldu to Bantam Bay, so do not be afraid to experiment with bait from worm/fish/crab/squid and even buttered kipper tied with elasticised cotton

Edible crab can be found along this stretch of coastline.

Pwlldu Bay

Hunts Bay to Bacon Hole
NGR 566/867

Bait	No

When you walk down the path from 'Hunts farm, at the bottom take the left hand path down to the rocky foreshore, and just where the rocks start to get higher you will see a stone and coarse sand gully at bottom water, it's the only bit of sand in the bay.

Fish off the top of the rocks here with a single hook crab trace, with or without rotten bottom. You need to cast 60 yards just slightly to the right clear of the seaweed beds onto coarse sand and flat rock. You are in the right place if there is a cave type shelter behind you, and you can cast off the top of it here.

Bass Venue towards top water

To the right of the bay Westwards, between deep slade and Bacon Hole cave *NGR 563/868* is a bottom water spring tide venue. You will need to travel light, everything you need on you.
N.B. The further West you go towards Bacon Hole cave, the more wary you will have to be regarding the state of the tide and your escape route back to Hunts Bay.

Distance casting out over kelp and rocks with single hook rotten bottom trace.

No bait locally.

Bacon Hole Cave

Directions

From the Severn Bridge area, follow signs to Swansea City Centre, County Hall and Sketty, Gower A4067, past St. Helens Cricket and Rugby ground on your right.

When you travel under the footbridge by Swansea University get into the right hand lane to the traffic lights. Turn right for Sketty, A4216, past Singleton Hospital on your right, up to the T-junction and mini roundabout, turn right and follow signs for Swansea Airport and Gower, A4118, up to the next T-junction. Turn left for Gower and Killay, through the next set of traffic lights, two mini roundabouts (OLCHFA Public House on your left) another set of traffic lights, then turning left at the next mini roundabout Gower and Airport, A4118. Driving up through Upper Killay over the cattle grid, take the left hand fork signposted Port Eynon/South Gower/and Oxwich, A4118.

After passing Swansea Airport, drive to a single house on the right hand side, turn left here signposted Kittle, drive to a T-junction down narrow lanes and turn right, Pennard $^3/_4$ mile. Drive on to Southgate, and at Pennard Golf Club turn left into Southgate Road, drive down to a roundabout and park in the National Trust car park.

There is a road going along to Hunts Farm *NGR 565/873*, there is a restricted parking notice on the road, but travel along the road to see the path down to Hunts Bay. The distance down the path from the farm is just under $^1/_4$ mile.

Hunts Bay

Foxhole Bay and Ravens Cliff Cove Pennard
Foxhole Bay NGR 553/871

Bait	No

Walk from the car park down a steep path through gorse and bramble to a very rocky foreshore, best area to fish is towards the left of the bay down a man made rough concrete type slipway covering an outfall pipe.

Fish directly in front of the end of the pipe casting over rocks 40 yards onto clean sand, a fast retrieve should clear you of the rocks.

Commence fishing 2 to 3 hours before top water. Garfish can be caught along this stretch, as can Bass.

The area left Eastwards towards Hunts Bay along the cliff path is nigh impossible trying to push your way through thick gorse bushes with fishing tackle.

Ravens Cliff Cove *NGR 546/873*

From the car park walk to the right westwards along the bridleway tarmac road for about 500 yards until you reach the 'Sleeping Policeman' (humps on the road) by the wooden posted Bridleway sign. Turn left here and look for the narrow path leading down a steep slope to the flatish type rocky foreshore, possibly the last fishable venue before Pobbles Bay.

Expect heavy tackle losses around both these venues.

Try crab at Ravens Cliff around bottom water, harbour rag and fish bait at Foxhole Bay.

Also try float fishing with live sand eel both venues.

Directions

The directions are the same as per Hunts Bay, parking in the National Trust Car Park.

Foxhole Bay

Another view of Foxhole Bay

Pobbles Bay and Shirecombe
NGR 541877

Bait	No

The walk to Pobbles from Shepherds shop is from a field opposite with a lane alongside MAES-Y-HAF house, take this path which takes you over a small bridge, turn right up through the woods and emerging down onto grass and sand.

Just under the road by Y FELIN DŴR craft centre runs the Ilston stream, which joins up with the Pennard Pill, this river runs curving through Pennard Burrows and emerging out between Pobbles and Three Cliffs Bay in to the sea. Walk tight to the left hand side beneath Pennard Castle, and you will come to Three Cliffs, under which is a natural archway which you can walk through, but exit sometimes will need thigh waders, or cross Pennard Pill, walk around in front of Three Cliffs to Pobbles.

But perhaps the safest way is up over the sand dunes and descend down to Pobbles Bay.

A surf/sandy beach with the best fishing starting about two hours before top tide, but try earlier fishing at the left hand side at Shirecombe, and follow the tide in back to the centre of Pobbles.

Fish two rods, one long range, one close, with worm baits, seeking out the roving Bass with paternoster and running ledger rigs.

Towards Hunts

Directions

Follow the directions as for Hunts Bay, page 37, up to Upper Killay, follow the A4118 into Parkmill. Stop at Shepherds shop and ask about parking for fishing at Pobbles Bay, sometimes in the summer parking is allowed in the field opposite alongside MAES-Y-HAF house. There will be a car park charge in the field.

Another way to Pobbles Bay is from the National Trust car park at Pennard, page 37. Walking to the right westwards along the bridle path until you descend down to Pobbles Bay with Pennard Golf Course on your right.

Both directions will be something in the region of one mile.

After the rocky shore from Mumbles along the coast to Pennard, now starts a fine stretch of sandy coastline. Be careful of fishing this venue because of Pennard Pill flooding behind you.

Pobbles

Heatherslade – Three Cliffs

NGR 534/877

Bait	No

Walk down the steep stoned stepped lane, and take note of the path to the right of the wooden slatted path, this path will take you up through the woods to fish the inner rocks marks. Try to arrive just after bottom water to check out the rock marks.

If fishing the beach, fish in front of the first sand dune. *NGR 535/879.* But there are a couple of excellent inner rock marks round to the right hand side, with the escape route at top water back through the woods.

Further round the Bay you will come to 'William Rock' cove, a large rock separated from the mainland at top tide. Try fishing this sloping sandy cove as the tide comes between the rocks. *NGR 533/877* SPRING TIDE.

There is no easy route back, the escape route at top water is up a steep sandy bank, along the headland and back down through the wooded area.

The Pennard Pill winds itself out to the sea to the left of the Bay, which will flood at high tide, so a little bit of common sense required when fishing these venues.

A wide variety of species to be caught here, Flounder/Plaice, with the possibility of Ray and Bream, plus the occasional Bass.

Try a variety of Baits, and if fishing off the rocks, try some peeler crab and Mussel tied on with thin elasticated cotton.

William Rock Cove – Three Cliffs

Directions

I will explain the way to Three Cliffs Bay coming from Cardiff or across the Severn Bridge areas, and the way to TOR BAY, which is just around the corner coming from the West Wales area.

Follow the signs to Swansea City centre, County Hall and Sketty/Gower A4067 past St. Helens Cricket and Rugby Ground on your right. When you travel under the road bridge by Swansea University, get into the right hand lane to the traffic lights, turn right for Sketty A42l6. Past Singleton Hospital up to the T-junction, and mini roundabout, turn right and follow the sign for Swansea Airport and Gower A4118, up to the next T-junction, turn left for Swansea Airport and Killay. Through the next set of traffic lights, two mini roundabouts, another set of traffic lights, then turning left at the next mini roundabout, Gower and Airport A4118, driving up through Upper Killay. Over the cattle grid, take the left hand fork signposted Port Eynon/South Gower/Oxwich A4118. Follow this road past Swansea Airport down through Parkmill, with the Gower Inn Public House on your right, then you will pass Shepherds shop and Y FELIN DŴR craft centre, up the hill until you reach Penmaen – park by the small St. John the Baptist Church on the grass verge. If this area is full drive, up the same road for about 300 yards and park by the National Trust sign for Cefn Bryn.

From the Church, cross the main road and walk opposite down the road 200/300 yards, then turn right down through NOTTHILL. There is NO parking along this stretch of road at any time. At the end of the road turn right by STONESFIELD holiday bungalows alongside the emergency 999 telephone.

Shirecombe – Pobbles – Three Cliffs

43

Tor Bay

NGR 529/877

Bait	No

The walk down to Tor Bay is signposted down the lane $^1/_2$ mile (0.8km), at the end of the lane after passing through the last gate, you will come to a small wooden right angle sign, Three Cliffs straight on, Tor Bay to the right.

(As a matter of interest, at the wooden sign, you will see a tree straight ahead – 70 yards away and a further 60 yards straight on, in an indent in the dunes, are the remains of the old Penmaen Church. To the right 60 yards away are the remains of the burial chamber of PEN-Y-CRUG, with the 7 ton lid left off after the excavation).

Walk across the burrows until you see the remains of an old brick built lime kiln, descend just before here to the sandy beach, or walk along to the left along the cliff path, some care needed. Walk along to the end beneath Great Tor but do not go around the corner, you will see some flat ledges, off which you can fish two hours before top water, casting onto clean sand. This mark is suitable for 4 anglers, fishing 2 up and 2 down off the rocks. Distance from the car park is over $^1/_2$ mile.

If you decide to park your car at the St. John the Baptist Church car park for Three Cliffs, follow the directions down to Three Cliffs, but instead of going up over the slatted path, turn right and climb up to the headland, and walk along the cliff path above Great Tor until you see the rounded brick lime kiln and the path down to the beach. This is a longer walk, something like $^3/_4$ mile or more. Tor Bay is a popular summer resort, so try fishing off the rocks either side of the bay.

Great Tor on the left – Little Tor on the right.

Tor Bay Lime kiln

Directions

I will explain the directions to TOR BAY from the Carmarthenshire area – Tor Bay is just along the coast from Three Cliffs.

From the Carmarthenshire areas, come off at Junction 47 (M4) and follow the sign Swansea A483 down to the roundabout, turn right onto the A484 Llanelli Road. Turn left at the sign Gowerton B4286, travel under the railway bridge, up the hill straight on through the traffic lights to the next set of traffic lights, turn left and after 100 yards take the right hand fork B4296 Dunvant/Killay. Up the hill at Dunvant, turn right at the garage down to a mini roundabout, turn right to Swansea Airport A4118 (you are now meeting up with the directions as if travelling from the Severn Bridge/Cardiff areas).

Drive up through Upper Killay over the cattle grid, take the left hand fork signposted Port Eynon/South Gower/Oxwich A4118. Follow the road past Swansea Airport down through Parkmill, with the Gower Inn public house on your right, passing Shepherds shop and Y FELIN DŴR craft centre, then up the hill until you reach Penmaen (parking here for Three Cliffs Bay see page 43). Drive a further $^4/_{10}$ mile to a small car park on the left hand side, just after Rose Cottage by the bus stop and the Royal Mail post box.

Tor Bay

Nicholaston Burrows/Crawley Woods

NGR 525/878

Bait	No

Cross the main road and walk down the road opposite, past Nicholaston Farm (farm shop open in the summer) follow the sign for Nicholaston Burrows ¼ mile (0.37km) down the wooden slatted path through the area known locally as Crawley Woods, follow the left hand path, a distance of ½ mile from the car park down to the beach.

Try fishing three hours from top water on the left hand side towards Little Tor, following the tide in along the front of the cliffs. No bait along this stretch of sandy bay.

Oxwich Bay is a popular holiday makers resort with lots of boat activity on the western end, whereas Nicholaston Burrows is on the extreme easterly side and has not quite so many holiday makers.

Try taking a small barbecue on a summer evening (towards top water), in the small sheltered inlet where the cliffs finish, and there is a single tree still standing behind you at this point. You might be lucky enough to catch a Bass or Mackerel.

Because Lug and Razor fish can be gathered at Oxwich, try a cocktail of lug tipped with fresh, not frozen, razor fish.

Nicholaston Cliffs –
note the single tree

Directions

Same as per Tor Bay. After passing the car park for Tor Bay, carry on for another $^3/_{10}$ mile to the Nicholaston sign on the left hand side of the road, and park behind the bus stop on the grass verge, just after the sign 'Beynon Nicholaston Farm'.

Site of Old
Penmaen Church

Nicholaston Burrows

Oxwich

NGR 512/848

Bait	Lug, Razor Fish, Crab

I will explain where to fish two venues, although you can fish the whole length of the sandy bay to Nicholaston Pill during quieter months of the year.

Venue 1 – Oxwich Point and Four Finger Bay Bottom water mark.

To fish this venue, you are facing something like a 1½ mile walk to the point, so tackle up accordingly, walk to the right hand side of the bay and when it gets slippery over the seaweed strewn rocks keep tight to the cliffs. You will pass the wreck of HMS Solar, visible at low water, also worth a try at this point casting with rotten bottom as near to the wreck as possible, trying to clear the seaweed and kelp, some tackle losses here.

When you reach Oxwich Point you will see to your left heavy kelp beds, nearly impossible to retrieve here with light weight tackle. Arrive at this location at bottom water, where you will see some 250 yards to the right a small bay with less kelp and a strip of sand going slightly to the right, it's some 6 to 8 yards wide, fish here following the tide in and trying to cast along the strip of sand.

Around 600 yards further round the headland before Lucas Bay and Holy Wash you will come to a bay with four finger like strips of sand running up to the cliff path. Fishing the right area if behind you on the hill are two look out posts. If you fish this venue nearly or up to top water, you will not be able to walk back along the beach, you will have to go up through the woods and down past St. Illtyd's Church. If you are losing gear, try a rotten bottom rig. All the summer species can be caught along this stretch of coastline. Take a shrimp net to forage amongst the rock pools and a crabbing hook.

War time look out post above 'Four Finger' Bay, Oxwich

48

Venue 2 – NGR 505/862

The corner of the bay from St. Illtyd's Church to the beach, bottom to top water, try off the rocks beneath the church in the woods, onto clean sand at 20 yards.

A point to note, fishing along the rocks to Oxwich Point, the tide will cover the rocks, but there are escape paths up through the woods and back down to the church. Ensure you know the whereabouts of one before you start fishing, that is if you intend to stay to around the top water mark.

Bait Gathering –

Razor fish can be collected at bottom water along the beach, also lug worm. Crab can be collected amongst the rocks around the Church area.

The best time for gathering Razor Fish is during the summer on a Spring tide but unfortunately they are being over picked.

Folly Castle Towers

Oxwich Castle

Oxwich Church

Directions

From the Cardiff/Severn Bridge area, follow the signs to Swansea City centre, Sketty/Gower A4067, past St. Helens Cricket and Rugby ground on your right. When you travel under the footbridge by Swansea University, take the right hand lane to the traffic lights. Turn right for Sketty A4216 up to a mini roundabout and T-junction, turn right and follow sign for Swansea airport and Gower A4118, up to next T-junction, turn left for Killay. Through the next set of traffic lights, two mini roundabouts, another set of traffic lights, then turning left at next mini roundabout Gower A4118, driving up through Upper Killay, over cattle grid, take the left hand fork signposted Port Eynon/South Gower/Oxwich A411R, past Swansea Airport, through Parkmill and Penmaen, until you reach the sign Oxwich/Slade. Turn left at Penrice 'The Folly Castle Towers', down the steep hill across Oxwich marsh passing Serpentine Broad Pool on your right (plenty of small rudd) to the Council owned car park. Drive to the foreshore turn right and park at the far end. There is a car park charge – free in winter, but boulders across entrance.

This is a very popular holiday makers beach with lots of boats and water sports.

A more scenic route but slightly longer is to carry on past the 'Folly' to the next left hand turn at Home Farm opposite the Granary House. Travel down 'Penny Hitch' lane up past Penrice Church and follow the signs for Oxwich, passing Pit Farm on the way.

Penrice Castle

51

Slade – Lucas Bay – Holywash
NGR 487/854

Bait	No

Try fishing the sandy area of beach in early spring before the holiday makers and surfers. Try using two rods if you can manage it, because of the run of the tide and lively surf, you will need waders and good long steady casts.

Use a one hook rig long range, try using crab and fish bait, and a paternoster with worm baits, switch baits until successful.

No digable bait here, perhaps a few Peeler Crab and small Mussel, although Edible Crab can be found along the stretch of rocks.

Towards Oxwich Point is Lucas Bay and Holy Wash NGR 495/853, the area with greyish white pebbles and small rock gullies (good offshore Plaice mark here), so try fishing the gullies until the tide makes it unfishable, with a rotten bottom rig and just one rod, crab bait for Bass. Expect heavy tackle losses.

You can fish this venue on a number of occasions with not a lot of success, but the odd occasion can prove very productive with a variety of species being caught.

* At Bottom water try the gully where the rocks go the furthest out to sea.

Slade

Directions

Same as for Oxwich, but carry on past Oxwich Bay car park to a small cross roads, drive straight across up Gander Street, (steep hill) past Greenways caravan park, follow the sign Slade Bay 1.37km.

Park on the grass verge by Channel View house, walk down the lane and turn left at the sign for Horton 1.31km, carry on down the lane and cross at the stile by the sign Slade Bay 1.14km.

The distance from Channel View to Slade Bay is just over $^1/_4$ mile.

There are a couple of access points to the sandy beach – one is by rope, sometimes the rope is removed, but the easiest is about 250 yards to the right, to descend down over the rocks to the beach.

Looking to Lucas Bay – Holywash – Oxwich Point

Horton

NGR 477/856

Bait	Only Small Mussel

Walk to the sandy beach past Horton Inshore Lifeboat station, then go left to the edge of the rocks. Out in the bay you will see two buoys between which is the wreck of the 'Ivanhoe', fish in front of the left hand buoy. Behind you will see two white houses and a house with red roof tiles, try here at bottom water just as the tide starts to make. Try using two rods, again with a mixture of baits.

Another venue is the cove *NGR 481/855* at high water. To fish this venue walk the cliff path past Sea Beach Nursing Home, and approximately 500 yards past the house with the red roof tiles, you will come to the access point to the 'cove' and the sloping rocks. Try some crab and shrimp tied on with elasticised cotton – Bass venue.

The problem with fishing Horton in the summer is that it is a popular holiday makers resort, so try on a cloudy/wet and overcast day, when there are not too many people about.

See Port Eynon regarding black and blow lug.

Horton inshore rescue station

Directions

Follow the signs through. Swansea on the A4067, until you travel under the footbridge by Swansea University, then take the right hand lane to the traffic lights, turn right for Sketty A4216 past Singleton Hospital, up to the T-junction and mini roundabout. Turn right and follow sign for Swansea Airport and Gower A4118 up to the next T-junction, turn left for Killay through the next set of traffic lights, two mini roundabouts, another set of traffic lights and turn left at the next mini roundabout, Gower A4118. Up through Upper Killay over the cattle grid and follow the sign for Port Eynon. Carry on past Swansea Airport, through Parkmill – Penmaen, past the castle Folly at the Oxwich turn off, straight on through Knelston. Follow the sign on the bend to Port Eynon A4118 straight on through Scurlage towards Port Eynon A4118 up the hill and watch for the sign 'Moor Corner Farm' on your right, and then take the left hand turn signposted Horton. Drive down the narrow road past the entrance to Bank Farm caravan site, then turn right signposted to Horton, drive through the village and park in the Pay and Display car park at the bottom of the hill. Free parking in the winter months.

Horton Bay

Eastwards over Horton Beach

55

Port Eynon – Culver Hole
NGR 475/854

Bait	Black and Blow Lug, Crab

The rocky venues first. Walk down to the foreshore and go right past the youth hostel, then at Salthouse ruins, walk straight out along the spit of sand to the sea. You have now passed the areas from the Youth Hostel known as – Inner Quay, Crowders Quay, Perchers Pools, Sedgers Bank with the grass top, nice spot for a barbecue, then Skysea. At Skysea turn right and walk a couple of hundred yards, to arrive at bottom water to fish the tide in off the flat rock surfaces.

There are a number of small rocky bays along this stretch of coastline, try the one between Skysea and Port Eynon Point *NGR 473/843*. You will see the East Helwick Buoy out in the bay to your right.

If you decide to visit the well known CULVER HOLE cave, it is easier to walk, with the appropriate footwear at bottom water along the flat rocks. There is a kelp bay directly in front of the cave, fishable two hours in from bottom water, casting out over the kelp beds.

The distance from the car park to Culver Hole Cave is just over one mile.

All this area is extremely rocky, so use just one rod, light as possible that will cast 4oz as far as possible, but one that can fish the gullies in close. You will have to use a rotten bottom rig, with crab being the most productive bait during the summer months.

Edible crab can be gathered along this stretch of coast in the crevices facing the sea.

Directions

The directions are as Horton – page 55, down to Scurlage, then carry straight on along the A4118 to a pay and display car park at Port Eynon. Free parking during the winter months. Some nice picnic tables around grassed areas.

Culver Hole

Port Eynon Bay *NGR 471/851*

Port Eynon Bay is very popular during the summer, and if you prefer to fish onto sand, fish the tide in on the right hand side around the curve of the rocks, casting to the left onto clean sand.

Black and Blow Lug can be dug/ pumped towards the middle of the bay at bottom water

Overton Mere

Bait	Very limited Crab and Mussel

Venue 1 – top water *NGR 464/848*

When you arrive at the foreshore you will see a concrete covered outfall pipe. Try and arrive at bottom water if fishing this venue for the first time, because just to the right of the pipe is a 100 yard stretch of a mixture of stone and sand straight out to part of a ships steel structure (The surfers call this area Sumpters point). Cast into this area towards top water – rotten bottom rig.

Venue 2 – bottom water *NGR 461/846*

Walk along the rocks for some 400/500 yards to the right, you will then come to flat rock right out to bottom water, with shelving towards the top water mark. With patches of broken sand down towards bottom water, at your back at this point is a pebble strewn cutting in the cliff below the path.

Venue 3 – Boiler plate reef *NGR 446/852*

To reach boiler reef means about a mile walk westwards towards Paviland along the cliff path, past Overton Cliff with the oblong type cave cut in the face. Then you will come to Longhole Lime Kiln, followed by Longhole Cave *NGR 452/850* – difficult to find. The cave is on the seaward side of the next cliff (someone has painted 41 alongside the opening). You will then come to Boiler Cliff, a rock climb with the flat face of the cliff facing you, south west if approaching from Paviland. At bottom water you will see a small curved section of a ships boiler protruding up from the rocks. Fish just to the left at this point at bottom water moving back up the reef to fish off flat rock and shingle until the tide takes over at the jagged pinnacle rocks.

Longhole Cave, Overton

58

Directions

Same as for Horton – page 55, through Scurlage on the A4118 to Port Eynon, then as you pass the NEWPARK CARAVAN PARK going down the hill, half way down you will see the sign to OVERTON. Drive down the narrow road to the sign OVERTON MERE 0.6 km. Very difficult parking around the village green area because of the boulders that have been placed alongside all grass verges. But park tight to the hedge on the left hand side after MAYBANK HOUSE just past the lane at the sign for Overton.

Walk down the lane, through the gateway (please close the gate) down through the valley, across the field – on the right you will see a row of beehives, if they are still there, down past the sewage water treatment works to the rocky foreshore of Overton, a distance of $^1/_4$ mile.

Overton

Paviland

Bait	No

Venue 1 – NGR 437/859

The rocky foreshore of Paviland is a spring tide venue, the higher the better. Tides of over 12 metres, Swansea tide table.

Fishing 1½ hours either side of bottom water, as you scramble down to the rocky foreshore to the left you will see some flat rocks towards. low water. Fish at this point and cast out over the kelp beds.

To the right at bottom water as you descend you will see a strip of sand, this area allows access to Paviland Cave, but be wary of the state of the tide.

This is a mainly Bass venue with single hook rigs and rotten bottom, try crab.

Venue 2 – Boiler Cliff *NGR 445/853*

As you descend down through Foxhole Slade pass, after you cross over the last stile, by the National Trust sign, turn left up over common cliff. Follow the path until you reach a gate with a step over stile alongside, at this point go to the right and walk along the cliff path until you reach a basin type valley, descend here and walk along the bottom path until you reach a smooth boulder bay/foreshore. Fish off the flat rocks at bottom water out over kelp and rocks, rotten bottom and long casting required. 500 to 600 yards further on towards OVERTON you will come to a narrow gully, fish off the rocks here at bottom water. Fine shingle along this gully on the bottom, nice place for a swim.

Then finally along the headland you will come to Boiler Plate Reef of flat rocks. *see OVERTON*

Try a roving type fishing session along this stretch 1½ hours either side of bottom water, at a number of marks. Possible high tackle losses, all along Paviland.

Starting from Overton Mere, then you have Slades Foot, Overton, Overton Cliff, Wash Slade, Willbower, Red Gut, Longhole Gut, Kilboidy and Blackhole Gut.

Venue 3 – The Knave *NGR 433/862*

As you descend down through Foxhole Slade pass, after crossing the last stile turn right Westwards up over the cliff towards the triangular rock of the knave and descend between HORSE CLIFF and THE KNAVE.

Fishing Flat Rocky Bay is a difficult rocky descent to fish at bottom water, and not advisable to fish alone. Try fishing to the left at the gully before KNAVE ROCK casting towards Cormorant Island in front of the Knave.

Venue 4 – Three Sisters and Red Chamber *NGR 428/864*

After passing the Knave carry on walking westwards along the cliff top path until you come to RAMSGROVE VALLEY, a deep cleft cut between the cliffs, come back slightly and go down the cliff path to the rocks. If you face Worms Head you will see a small cave/hole in the rocks, fish the gully here at bottom water with rotten bottom, try a variety of baits, and if the gully has sufficient water try a plug. This is a pebbly cove.

There are one or two venues further along this stretch known locally as Three Sisters – three pinnacles of cliff.

There is easy access to Ramsgrove Valley if you stay at Pitton Cross Caravan Park.

Edible crab can be found amongst the rocks around Paviland.

The famous Paviland cave

From Paviland Rocks up over Common Cliff

61

Remains of winching gear

Remains of boiler plate

Directions

Travelling through Swansea on the A4067 past St. Helens Cricket and Rugby ground on your right. When you travel under the footbridge by Swansea University, take the right hand lane to the traffic lights. Turn right for Sketty A4216 past Singleton Hospital up to a T-junction and mini roundabout, turn right and follow the sign for Swansea Airport and Gower A4118, up to the next T-junction. Turn left for Killay, through the next set of traffic lights, two mini roundabouts and another set of traffic lights, turn left at the next mini roundabout Gower A4118. On through Upper Killay over the cattle grid and follow the sign for Port Eynon A4118. Carry on past Swansea Airport, through Parkmill and Penmaen, straight on past the Castle Folly (known locally as the Towers), at the Oxwich turn off, carry on to Knelston and follow the sign on the bend for Port Eynon A4118. Through Scurlage, then turn right to Rhossili B4247 past the Countryman Public House, (set your mileometer here, it is 1.3 of a mile to the parking area from here, any further and you have gone too far) drive past the small Emmanuel chapel, and Pitton Green Farm and then on the left you will see a large house on its own called CLIFFLANDS.

Park opposite just off the lane on the grass verge by the National Trust sign, at PILTON GREEN.

Cross the road climb over a stile with the sign Paviland Cave 1.6km, then walk through six fields on the right hand side, crossing over stiles and a small wooden bridge. You will then descend down through the rocky Foxhole Slade pass to the very rocky foreshore, which is just under a mile from the car park.

The Knave and Bull & Calf Rocks

Mewslade Bay
NGR 421/871

Bait	No

After parking the car at Pitton Farm, walk down the lane and follow the sign for Mewslade Bay, 0.85km, down past Wrinkle Tor Resting Bank Rock, with the view down the valley. Just as you arrive at the narrow entrance to the beach, climb over the stile on your left and walk around the cliff path, take care walking around the headland, stout boots required.

Best area to fish is off the rocks directly beneath Thurba Head, and when you look to the West you will see the flat rocks of Jackys Tor (another good venue) and directly in line with Lewes Castle Cliff, with Tears Point in the distance, Fishing on to clean sand.

Mewslade is a popular summer holiday makers beach, so if you intend trying the beach for Bass, try bottom water spring tide on an overcast or wet day, or early September.

The Bay has a wide expanse of sand at bottom water, but as the tide comes in you will be forced back to a narrow rock gully at top water.

Crab is the most successful bait off the rocks, with a mixture of worm baits being the most productive off the beach.

From Thurba Head overlooking the rocks of Three Sisters towards The Knave

Directions

From West Wales and the Severn Bridge, come off the motorway at junction 47, and follow the sign Swansea A483 down to the roundabout, turn right on the A484 Llanelli road. Then left at the sign Gowerton B4296. Travel under the railway bridge, up the hill, go on the outside lane to turn right at the traffic lights, Gower/Llanridian B4295. Straight on past a mini roundabout and through the traffic lights, travel down through Penclawdd – Crofty to Llanridian. Turn left at the general store and petrol station on to the B4271, sign to Swansea, past the north Gower Hotel on your right, on to the first junction. Turn right at the sign Cefn Bryn and Reynoldston, past Broad Pool on your right, up and over the hill of Cefn Bryn (with King Arthur's Stone over to the right) down through Reynoldston, with the King Arthur public house on your left, to a T-junction. Turn right for Port Eynon A4118 straight on through Knelston, follow the sign for Port Eynon and when you travel through Scurlage, turn right at the sign for Rhossili B4247. Past the 'Countryman' public house. Then on to Pilton Green, past Pitton Cross caravan park – watch for some farm buildings and a cross roads sign, turn left down the lane in front of you and park in Farmers Field. Honesty Box charge.

Another parking place for Mewslade is to travel on towards Rhossili past the small Wesleyan Chapel for $^4/_{10}$ of a mile until you reach Middleton, then first right at the telephone box, and park on the side of the road by Middleton Farm. Cross the main road, turn left, walk 100 yards then turn right just after the sign for Middleton down a narrow lane, through the gate and down a steep bank. (*There is a fig tree here on the right and a small vine yard in Farmers Field up the bank behind you*) to meet up with the path coming from Farmers Field.

On the hill going up to Cefn Bryn, near the top on the left hand side, is a small brick building housing a spring called 'LADYS WELL' owned now by Welsh Water calling it HOLY WELL' service reservoir.

This spring goes underground making its way down to feed BROAD POOL.

Falls Bay
NGR 414/873

Bait	No

Cross the main road, walk to the right down the lane past Rhossili Parish Hall, down through three farm fields. In the fourth field climb down a steel ladder, down the sloping grass banks, past the lime kiln to Falls Bay, which only has a stretch of sand some 300 yards long, with rocks at high water.

Some decent Bass are caught just a short distance off shore at this point by the small boats.

Distance from Middleton to Falls is $\frac{1}{2}$ mile. Popular holiday makers beach in the summer, so at the lime kiln you will see a path going over the cliff known as 'Lewes Castle' on your left. Walk along the cliff top path towards Mewslade, where midway you will come across Vould Lime Kiln NGR 416/873. Descend at this point between 'Double Valley Pass' down to Devil Truck Rocks, and Bass fish into deep water.

Falls Bay from the Lime Kiln

Directions

You can come off the M4 motorway at junction 47, as per directions for MEWSLADE, or travel through Swansea City centre following the sign Gower A4067 past St. Helens Cricket and Rugby ground on your right, and when you travel under the footbridge by Swansea University, get into the right hand lane to the traffic lights. Turn right for Sketty A4216 up to a mini roundabout, turn right and follow the sign for Swansea Airport and Gower A4118. Up to the next T-junction turn left for Gower and Killay. Through the next set of traffic lights, two mini roundabouts, another set of traffic lights, turn left at the next mini roundabout Gower A4118, on through Upper Killay and over the cattle grid and follow the sign for Port Eynon – still on the A4118. Follow this road through Parkmill – Penmaen through Knelston, and as you go around the bend you will see the sign for Port Eynon. Drive through Scurlage, then take the right hand turn to Rhossili B4247, past the 'Countryman' public house, driving through Monkstone, Pylewell, Pitton until you arrive at Middleton. After the Middleton sign take the first right by the telephone box and park on the grass verge.

From Tears Point over Falls Bay towards Lewes Castle

Rhossili Ledges to Kitchen Corner

Bait	No

To get to the flat rock ledges above the sea, walk down the lane past the coastguard station for about $^1/_4$ mile, there are a number of steep path descents on the right hand side to the ledges, walk along the cliff top and you will see the winding paths going down.

There is a boat house built on Kitchen Corner known as 'COONANS BOAT HOUSE, the more popular ledges are closest to this point.

To get to Coonans Boat House, walk to the end at Kitchen Corner alongside the empty lookout building, which has a 999 phone, and walk down the steep cliff path to fish alongside the boat house off the slope. I would not recommend fishing off the wooden winching platform between the two posts, the planks are rotten.

You are now fishing 122 miles from Lands End.

On a Spring tide, have a walk at bottom water from Rhossili beach to the boat house, to check out your favoured ledge and pick up some tackle.

The ledges are as follows from the boat house:
>   1st   The COVE – NGR 402/875, rocks for 20 yards then clean sand
>   2nd PILLAR LEDGE – NGR 403/876, clean sand
>   3rd   TERRACE LEDGE – NGR 404/877, clean sand
>   4th   SHEEPDROP LEDGE – NGR 405/878, clean sand
>   5th   PINNACLE LEDGE – NGR 406/879, clean sand

This is a popular summer and winter venue, with a lot of fishing being carried out during the hours of darkness, and a wide variety of species are caught, with a number of nice eels being taken.

The weather here is unpredictable, sea mists and fog can roll in, so take sufficient food and appropriate clothing.

Directions

I will explain the way to Rhossili Ledges from the West Wales area, and if you are travelling from the Severn Bridge areas it is the same as Rhossili Bay, page 75.

Come off the M4 motorway at junction 47, and follow the sign for Swansea A483 down to the roundabout, turn right on the A484 Llanelli Road, then left at the sign Gowerton B4296. Up to the set of traffic lights, drive straight on to another set of lights, turn left and after 100 yards take the right hand fork B4296 Dunvant/Killay up the hill through Dunvant, turn right at the garage down to a mini roundabout. Turn right Swansea Airport A4118 (you are now meeting up with the directions as if travelling from the Severn Bridge area).

Drive up through Upper Killay over the cattle grid and take the left hand fork signposted Port Eynon/South Gower & Oxwich A4118. Continue along this road through Parkmill, Penmaen, straight on past the 'Castle Folly' at Oxwich, and when you travel through Knelston, on the bend you will see the sign for Port Eynon. Follow this road through Scurlage, then take the right hand turn to Rhossili B4247 past the 'Countryman' public house, driving through Monksland, Pylewell, Pitton, Middleton and so to Rhossili.

Park at Worms Head Hotel car park, attendant summer £2.00, free in winter.

Coonans Boat House

Worms Head Rhossili

Bait	Crab

To fish the Worm, the first port of call is the tourist information shop, for safe crossing times, which they have in the Foyer, it is approximately $2^{1}/_{2}$ hours either side of low water, after which the tide will cover the causeway, and you will have to remain on the island until the tide retreats.

Walk down the lane past the old rocket launching apparatus pole, then along the fairway to the empty look out post at Kitchen Corner, then down to Shipway rocks – allow about 20 minutes from the Hotel to this point. If you arrive at these rocks about 3 hours after top tide, you can cross as the tide uncovers the rocks.

Soft and Peeler Crab can be collected at Shipway rocks, but as the Worm is so popular during the summer, it is advisable to bring some bait with you. (Crab rating Soft 6, Peeler 7, Hermit 8.)

There are numerous rock marks to fish off the Worm. On the southerly side off both corners of 'low neck' bay. The middle of 'low bay has lots of snag gullies and seaweed covered rocks and the westerly tip of the Worm is a little precarious off the rocks. You are unable to traverse around the point of the Worm at bottom water. So I will suggest two venues and leave you to explore the rest.

Venue 1 – Devils Bridge *NGR 388/878*

Just before you reach Devils Bridge, go down the rocks on the right hand side (northerly) to be able to fish off the rocks with crab, if the seals will give you some peace!

Venue 2 – Flat Plateau Bay *NGR 398/874*

After crossing the causeway over shipway rocks on the right hand side, go up to the flat grassy plateau and cast into the bay towards Burry Holmes.

So start fishing at *venue 1* and try a couple of hours at *venue 2* whilst waiting to cross back over to the mainland.

Worms Head showing Devils Bridge

Looking back over Devils Bridge

71

Tears Point

NGR 411/871

Bait	No

The walk is a continuation as for Rhossili Ledges, up to Kitchen Corner along the headland path and past the stone building (now empty). Carry on alongside the dry stone walling to descend down by the small boats which are up on the grass banks.

Walk to the right to Tears Point and fish off the flat rocks towards top water.

Try two rods, float fish one with crab close in. Cast the other out towards Lewes Castle at Falls Bay. Try using any cocktail type bait, switch to rotten bottom rig if you keep getting snagged. Good Bass venue.

The distance from Worms Head Hotel car park to Tears Point is just over 1 mile, you can also get to this venue from Middleton, see Falls Bay.

Falls Bay and Tears Point from the Lime Kiln

Directions

The same as for Rhossili Ledges

Mewslade towards Falls Bay

Pillar Rock

Rhossili Bay to the Old Rectory
NGR 411/882

Bait	Black Lug & some Razor Fish

The walk down to the beach is on the right hand side of the hotel signposted down a steep incline. (Popular hang gliding take off point up SLENT path to the top of rolling TOR)

The area to fish is between the wreck of the HELVETIA, timbers visible on the beach, and in amongst the coves to the left beneath the Rhossili cliffs by the wreck of the VERANI.

Some black Lug available in this vicinity at bottom water but not enough for professional bait diggers, just enough to supplement your other bait.

This is a big surf beach, and if the surfers are in the vicinity move across and fish in front of the old Rectory, the house on the hill towards the middle of the bay.

Main quarry Bass, with summer Mullet and some big Flounders. Probably the most used bait here is harbour ragworm, piled onto a two hook trace. (See harbour ragworm digging – Loughor page 109)

Try this venue anytime on the incoming tide.

Rhossili – Llangennith beach is one bay and the distance from the car park to Spaniards Rocks at Burry Holmes is about 2½ miles.

Two wrecks on Rhossili Bay, Helvetia and Verani

Directions

From the Severn Bridge areas. Travelling along the M4 motorway, cross over the new Briton Ferry bridge, take the Swansea turn off along Fabian Way on the A4067. Travel through Swansea, follow the sign Sketty/Gower, passing St. Helens Cricket and Rugby ground, when you travel under the footbridge by Swansea University, get into the outside lane to the traffic lights and turn right for Sketty A4216. Up to the T-junction and mini roundabout, turn right for Swansea Airport and Gower A4118, up to the next T-junction. Turn left for Gower and Killay, through the next set of lights, two mini roundabouts, another set of traffic lights, turn left at the next mini roundabout Gower A4118. On through Upper Killay and over the cattle grid, and follow sign for Port Eynon A4118, down through Parkmill/Penmaen straight on past the 'Castle Folly' at Oxwich, through Knelston, and on the bend after this, you will see the sign Port Eynon, drive through Scurlage, Then take the right turn to Rhossili B4247 past the 'Countryman' public house, driving through Monksland, Pylewell, Pitton, Middleton and so to Rhossili.

Park in the Worms Head Hotel car park, attendant summer, free in winter.

Rhossili Bay

75

Llangennith Bay/Hill End/Diles Lake/Spaniard Rocks

Bait	No

I will explain three of the top venues fishing along Llangennith Bay with the National Grid Reference Numbers.

Venue 1

When you arrive on the foreshore by the National Trust sign, turn left and walk approximately 900 yards to a big boulder on the beach and directly in front of the peak of hanging sker by Sweynes Howes Burial Chamber. *NGR 415/898.*

* Record Welsh Bass caught here

Venue 2

At the National Trust sign, walk to the right passing Diles Lake (river running into the sea) and half a mile from Burry Holmes is the wreck of the 'City of Bristol', visible only at bottom water. *NGR 399/925.*

* Record Welsh Golden Grey Mullet caught here.

Try fishing *venue 1* and *2*, two hours either side of top water.

Venue 3

Walk to Burry Holmes and to 'Spaniard Rocks', try to arrive at bottom water, walk to the point as close to the rocks as possible. Watch for the first run as the tide comes swirling in through small gullies and rocks. Fish into this swirl as long as possible with crab and harbour ragworm. *NGR 399/925*

One of the top surf beaches on the Peninsula with Bass again the main species, but also good catches of Flounder and Mullet. The beach appears to be almost devoid of any marine life, except for some Bi valve venus clams, (also called butterfish) just below the sand surface at bottom water.

Top baits – Harbour ragworm, Blow Lugworm. Surfing popular all the year.

Directions

From the West Wales and the Severn Bridge areas, come off at junction 47 (M4). Follow the Swansea road sign A483 down to the roundabout, turn right along the road signposted A484 towards Llanelli. Follow this road until you see the sign for GOWERTON, turn left here onto the B4296, travel under the railway bridge, up the hill, get into the outside lane to turn right at the traffic lights. Gower/Llanridian B4295 straight on past a mini roundabout, then straight on at the traffic lights. Driving down through Penclawdd, Llanridian, Oldwalls and after passing the 'Greyhound' public house, bear left on the Llangennith road, follow this all the way through BURRY GREEN, along the winding narrow road until you reach Llangennith. After passing the 'Kings Head' public house carry straight on for a couple of hundred yards, and turn left at the mini roundabout sign posted HILL END, follow this road along to Hill End Camping and Static Caravan site.

Attendant parking during the summer, free in winter. Drive straight down and park at the end of the road, by the narrow entrance to the beach.

Diles Lake

Wreck of the City of Bristol

Burry Holmes

NGR 397/925

Bait	No

Arriving at the beach by the National Trust sign, walk to the right to Burry Holmes, a distance of one mile.

When you arrive at Spaniard Rocks before the small causeway, go up over the plateau, passing on your right the ruins of a Church Hall and old Chapel. When you arrive at the end, on the western side you will see a steel ring set in a circle of concrete, this is where the automatic light was sited after Whitford lighthouse was abandoned, go left here down a tricky descent to some flatish rock ledges towards the tip of the Holmes.

Also try float fishing between the two outcrops of rock, wear dark clothing as if Trout fishing, the Bass are in close.

Fishing to the right of the Holmes at the end is possible for the more fool hardy because the descent to the sea is extremely precarious, and fishing from the top you are too high up above the water.

NB. This venue is NOT recommended for the inexperienced or young fisherman or woman.

The Holmes becomes an island at top water, being cut off some 2½ hours either side of top water.

A wide variety of species can be caught off the Holmes. Mullet, Mackerel, Scad, Bass, Garfish etc. A variety of baits is recommended. It is also worth trying with a light rod and a plug of your choice.

Volme Cave

Directions

Are the same as for Llangennith.

Volme Bay

If you have youngsters with you and decide not to fish the Holmes *(it's not safe for children because of the climb down and around the rock areas)*, an excellent little venue is the sandy Volme bay, just after the small causeway, fish the incoming tide off the beach. Then climb on to the rocks right opposite the single pillar of the old ruined chapel, and fish into the causeway, where the Bass will be coming through in search of food.

Use crab off the rocks and plenty of harbour ragworm off the beach. *NGR 402/927*

Off Burry Holmes –
Volme Bay causeway, 1956

2006

Blue Pool/Three Chimneys/Minor Point/Broughton
NGR 409/930

Bait	No

Descending down the cliff path at bottom water you will see a large circular pool, some 18 feet in diameter and it is 12 feet deep. This is the 'Blue Pool' which gives its name to the venue, a popular swimming pool for the children in summer and not quite as cold as the sea.

Try fishing off the beach at bottom water into the surf, but as the tide starts to make, your escape will be cut off by the shear cliffs, so allow yourself plenty of time to climb around the back of Blue Pool, and fish just to the right of the life buoy off the rocks. (A word of caution here, if you hook a good Bass, the tendency is to go down the rocks to get him in – DON'T – the waves will pull you in if you get caught. It's best to play the fish and bring him in on a wave).

Cast towards three chimneys facing you around the bay, casting over the rocks onto clean sand.

Bait – crab, fishing three hours either side of top water.

Minor Point is reached by going further round to the right and down along the sloping rocks, try float fishing into the gullies. *NGR 409/932*

On a high spring tide it is possible at bottom water to walk from the bay at Broughton, past Twic Point, Minor Point, Blue Pool, Three Chimneys, Culver Hole to Spaniards Rocks and Burry Holmes.

Twic Point
Cove

Directions

From West Wales and Severn Bridge areas, come off at junction 47, follow the Swansea sign A483 down to the roundabout, turn right signposted A484 to Llanelli. Follow this road until you see the sign for Gowerton, turn left on to the B4296, travel under the railway bridge, up the hill, get into the outside lane to turn right at the traffic lights Gower/Llanridian B4295 straight on past a mini roundabout, through the traffic lights, driving down through Penclawdd, Llanridian, Oldwalls and after passing the 'Greyhound Inn public house, bear left on the Llangennith road. Follow this all the way through Burry Green, along the winding narrow road until you reach Llangennith After passing the 'Kings Head' public house drive straight down to a mini roundabout, go straight across and follow the sign BROUGHTON one mile.

Park in the field just before the entrance to Broughton Farm Caravan park (there will be a fee during the summer months).

Walk onto the caravan site, take the first left path, and the next left until you come to the cliff path and the sign BLUE POOL 1km. There is a nice wooden slatted path to the top, you will see TWIC POINT COVE to your right. At the top follow the right handed path and you will see two steel posts in the distance, they have a Blue Pool danger sign attached. Go down the cliff at this point.

Distance from the car park is about half a mile.

Blue Pool

'Tortoise Rock'
Near Three Chimneys

Twic Point and Foxhole Point, Broughton

Bait	No

Twic Point *NGR 416/932*

Twic Point is reached by taking the first left after entering Broughton Bay Farm caravan park, then straight on until you come to the cliff path around the headland, to a steep descent to a nice cove of clean sand and stones.

Use harbour ragworm two hours either side of top water for Flounder and Bass in the summer. With Black Lug and Fish bait for Dab/Dogfish and Flounder with the occasional School Bass in the winter months.

Foxhole Point *NGR 413/933*

Foxhole Point is a difficult fishing venue off the rocks, but check this out first at bottom water spring tide, but I would recommend that you travel on to fish Blue Pool, being much more productive.

Cave near Foxhole Point

Minor Point

Broughton Bay

83

Llanmadoc Side of Broughton Bay
and *Whitford Lighthouse* (built in 1866)
NGR 434/947

Bait	Black Lug, Razor Fish, Crab

When you emerge onto the beach, walk straight down to fish two hours either side of bottom water preferably on a spring tide. Out in the bay you will see a sand bank, this is Lynch Sands. The tide comes in from Burry Holmes, through the south channel past Lynch and Hooper sands, through the Burry Inlet and in to the Loughor Estuary.

Behind you and slightly to the left you will see two caves up on Prissons Tor Cliff.

Main species in the summer: Flounder/Bass and Tope have been caught coming through the channel. Dab/Flounder/Dogfish in the winter.

Whitford Lighthouse area NGR 442/967

Fishing the Whitford Lighthouse area, approximately 800 yards before the lighthouse at bottom water, you will come to a curve in the rocks, like a small bay.

Good Bass mark July/September. Mussels/Soft and Peeler crab can be gathered here.

Small lake at Broughton

Directions

From West Wales and Severn Bridge areas come off at junction 47 on the M4 motorway, follow the Swansea sign A483 down to the roundabout and turn right on the A484 to Llanelli. Follow this road until you see the sign for Gowerton. Turn left onto the B4296, travel under, the railway bridge, up the hill, get into the outside lane to turn right at the traffic lights Gower/Llanridian B4295, straight on past a mini roundabout, through the traffic lights, driving down through Penclawdd/Crofty to Llanridian. Straight on past the garage and Llanridian Primary School, then when you pass the. 'Greyhound Inn public house, take the right hand fork to LLANMADOC along the narrow road past WEOBLEY CASTLE to CHERITON. Past the 'Britannia Inn' and straight on to the sign Broughton Beach, but take the right hand fork before the Church of St. Madoc, and half way down the hill park in a farmer's field with an Honesty Box parking at Cwm Ivy.

Walk down the narrow road, through the gate onto Forestry Commission property, and at the bottom of the hill you will see amongst the pine trees 'BURROWS COTTAGE', two paths lead to the beach at this point. One is a path up over the hill, and the other is through the gate, turn left immediately and through the woods to the beach, walking alongside the wire fence.

Whitford Lighthouse

Whitford continued
Berges Island – The Groose

Bait	Blow Lug and Poor Ragworm

Venue 1 – NGR 452/964

Walk to the left of the Bird look out station along the sand until you come to the corner of the sand dunes, fish the tide in towards the mouth of the BURRY PILL.

Venue 2 – NGR 453/962

Approximately 500 yards to the left of the Bird station, casting into the estuary with the tide running to your right.

Venue 3 – NGR 454/961

200 yards to the right of the Bird station off the sand, with the reed marshes on your right, casting along the gully mouths.

Lugworm can be dug out on the sand towards Burry Pill. There are only poor Ragworm and the Pills are treacherous if digging on your own, so take care, deep mud.

There used to be four Public Houses in Llanmadoc, the 'Britannia Inn', the 'Farmers Arms' then to become the 'Danes Dyke' which burnt down and is now rebuilt as a private dwelling. 'The Old Ship' and 'The Mariners'. Now only one remains, the Britannia Inn.

Towards Berges Island from Llanridian

Whitford *continued*

To fish Berges Island, drive past the 'Britannia Inn public house, around the corner and park on the hill left hand side on the grass verge just after the dead end sign.

The access to the lane is opposite where there is a slow sign painted on the road and alongside GLENSIDE COTTAGE. Walk down the lane past the two white washed cottages, 'Pill House' and 'Pill Cottage', over the wooden stiles with the specially built lifting posts for dog access.

Out onto Whitford Trust National Nature reserve, follow the path and head towards the rounded clump of pine trees in the distance. As you approach the trees you will see a shed type building on your right, this is an ornithologists bird watching station. Do not try and take a short cut to the pine trees across the deep muddy pills, but keep to the path, and midway between the bird look out and pine trees turn right out to the marsh. The distance from the car to the pine trees at Berges Island is $2^{1}/_{2}$ miles. Another way out to Berges Island is through the woods at Cwm Ivy past 'Burrows Cottage'.

It is an open windswept, sandy location with Bass being the main species. There are numbers of fishable venues, but I will suggest three in relation to the bird station.

But take note that Burges Island is an estuary and there is NO water until mid water mark, and on a spring tide there is a strong run past Whitford lighthouse, up in to the Burry Pill and to the Groose. So fish a tide something between 10.6 and 11.2 metres.

Yellow Bank with Whitford
Lighthouse in background

Whitford Lighthouse *continued*

300 yards past Whitford Lighthouse, you come to a stretch of sand with a sloping bay, try and fish close to the edge of the stones, fishing the tide in. Start at bottom water into the gully, and as the tide makes, work your way right, fishing off a sand bar known as 'Yellow Bank'.

Blow Lug available here.
NGR 446/974

Try the walk back from here to Cwm Ivy along the National Trust path. Past the area known as Berges Island, through the pine forest passing the woodmans hut and finally up the hill to Cwm Ivy.

If you pick some mussels from Whitford around September, do not be surprised to find some small orange striped crabs living quite happily inside the shell of the mussel.

Pea Crab that live inside Mussel

Broughton Bay continued

The Gower Society have written an article about a medieval fish weir by Quentin Kay and Melvyn Davies, Issue No XLIV, situated at Whitford Sands – *NGR 442/955.*

It is made up of timbers driven into the blue clay and mud in a V formation, with the point facing north, and they have had the timbers dated at AD 1210 and AD 1330.

The odd thing about this is after all this time someone has erected two scaffold type frames with ropes between and spikes spliced into the ropes with the buoys marked *Coastline Mussels 0267,* and they are positioned directly in front of the weir. Both visible at bottom water spring tide. Although the outer one has been damaged by the January storms of '97, and probably both will have vanished within a couple of years.

The Burry Inlet is a Bass Nursery area with a complete ban on Bass fishing from boats, area 19, which is from the lighthouse area all the way up to Loughor, May to October – this is to include rod and nets.

Whitford Lighthouse – The first lighthouse was built on a pile like structure in 1854. Then the existing tower – which is the only cast iron lighthouse in the country – was built in 1866 by HENNETT & CO. for £1600, it was superseded by the light on Burry Holmes on the 21st December, 1921.

Broughton Bay

Landimore Marsh

NGR 461/940

Bait	Poor Lugworm, Limited Crab

Fishing the Landimore man made pill. I mention this venue for some fun fishing on a warm June/July day on a tide height of between 10.3 and 10.6 metres – Swansea Tide Table.

Walk-up some 500 yards along the man made pill and float fish for Bass, gold fish to trout size, on small river tackle, with hooks of 4 to 6 and 4 to 5lb line. Fishing in the pools with small Ragworm, if the small Bass are there you will see them playing along the top of the water.

Try fishing half an hour either side of top water, with the float about 4" to 6"above the hook, and leave to drift down stream like trout fishing, sit on the left hand side of the bank to cast.

There is some Flounder fishing in the winter months on a low tide, where the man made pill meets the Great Pill coming from the right hand side NGR 460/943, but you will be cut off by the tide with a number of deep muddy gullies. So take extreme care, and I do not recommend you fish this venue.

Man made Pill at Landimore

Directions

As per Broughton Bay

After the Greyhound public house take the right hand turning, sign posted Weobley Castle, Landimore and Llanmadoc. After you pass the entrance to the castle (worth a visit) it is $^8/_{10}$ of a mile to the right hand turn to Landimore.

Drive down the narrow road past the dead end sign, passing the telephone box and BOVEHILL, to park on the grass verge by the National Trust sign CORS Landimore marsh.

Pass through the gate and walk down the stone strewn path, with TOR GRO cliffs on your left, until you come to some small boats moored at the end of Bennets Pill. At this point there is a man made river running straight out to sea.

It is difficult to believe when driving through Landimore that it once had a school, shops, three public houses and a small port. All gone!

A note of caution, when fishing any of the marsh areas, only fish on a low tide, something like 10.6 metres on the Swansea tide table, and never fish alone on an unknown venue. Also seek knowledge regarding the conditions, and be aware of the dangers.

Accidents have happened along the river Loughor.

From the Groose – with Pill House and Pill Cottage in the background

Weobley Castle

NGR 473/949

Bait	No

No fishing along this stretch of coast line. There is a private road going out along the causeway from Weobley Castle. But out in the Bay is a look out post used by the Americans during the 1939-45 war. It is built on concrete legs and has a brick-work shelter.

Walking out along the causeway there is a mound on the right hand side, this where the barracks were sited, and to the left of this point is another old fish weir, *(not as old as the one near Whitford Lighthouse)* with the stakes just protruding above the ground.

The distance from the castle to the look out post is 1¹⁄₄ miles.

Weobley Castle

Directions

See Landimore

Park in Weobley Castle grounds.

American lookout post on Llanridian Marsh

Wernffrwd

NGR 515/942

Bait	Lug

To fish Wernffrwd is an approximately one mile walk out along the cart track, and across the marsh grass to the edge of the sand. Arrive just as the tide starts to make. Fish the area as the tide comes round the bend in a zig-zag fashion towards the boat guidance post, approximately 500 yards to the right.

Because of the tidal race of the estuary, as a precautionary measure, until you familiarise yourself with the area, only fish this venue on a low tide, something in the region of 10.6 metres on the Swansea tide table.

Mainly Flounder, Bass & Eels in the estuary. Try crab during the summer, and later on in the year use harbour ragworm and lugworm.

Lugworm can be dug out on the sand/mud flats.

Grass/Mud banks at Penclawdd

Directions

Come off at junction 47 on the M4 motorway, follow the Swansea sign A483 down to the roundabout, then right on the A484 to Llanelli. Follow this road until you see the sign for Gowerton, turn left on to the B4296. Travel under the railway bridge, up the hill, get into the outside lane to turn right at the traffic lights Gower/Llanridian B4295. Straight on past a mini roundabout, through the traffic lights driving down through Penclawdd, and after the Crofty Industrial Estate turn off, take the next right down PENCAER FENNI lane and signposted CROFTY. Drive down the narrow road past the 'Crofty Inn' public house, across the small Morlais river road bridge out onto Gors Llanridian marsh.

Drive along the narrow coast roadway and park by the small St. Davids Church on the left hand side. Opposite this church is the track that leads out to the cockle beds.

The coast road is liable to flooding during a spring tide. Extreme care is required out on the marsh.

Marsh Samphire

95

Slipway

Bait	Lug, Crab, Limited Ragworm

After parking look towards the sea, and in front of you is the 'long arm' of the slipway – a man made structure of boulders and rocks. Walk out to the end of the slipway and then down slightly left to the sea, you will come to a break in the rocks, (at bottom water). These rocks run the whole length of this stretch of the estuary and nigh impossible to reel the weight in up and over when the tide is in.

NGR 519/963 Fish at this point at the start of the tide, it is a low tide venue owing to the tidal race up the Burry Inlet. Fish until the water comes up over the rocks.

Flounder, Eels, Bass during the summer months. Crab troublesome so use crab, and frequent checking of bait if using worm. Mainly Flounder winter months.

The three fastest tidal races (Bore) in the World are:

> *No.1   Bay of Sunday (Canada)*
>
> *No.2   The River Severn (Bristol Channel)*
>
> *No.3   The Yangtze (China)*

> * *The Burry Estuary is also extremely fast. Possibly second to the river Severn in this Country, but it has no bore as such.*
>
> *The estuary almost empties and refills on each tide, just the river remains.*

Directions

Come off at junction 47 on the M4 motorway, follow the Swansea sign A483 down to the roundabout, turn right on the A484 to Llanelli. Follow this road until you see the sign for Gowerton, turn left onto the B4296, travel under the railway bridge, up the hill, get into the outside lane to turn right at the traffic lights Gower/Llanridian B4295, straight on past a mini roundabout, through the traffic lights drive down through Penclawdd, then watch for the turn off to Crofty Industrial Estate on the right, before the Pencaer Fenni turn off.

Drive down through the Industrial Estate to the big roundabout, and park on the right hand side.

If you decide to fish this location on a high tide, fish at the end of the 'Slipway', at the point where there is a slope of concrete, casting out over the lugbeds two hours either side of top water. Best fishing later on in the year.

Two rod venue with a variety of baits, try some crab and mussel whipped on with the thinnest of elasticated cotton.

Lug can be dug on the firm sand just off the end of the slipway, some small harbour ragworm still remain to the left of the slipway in the gullies – but poor.

Crab can be collected at low water amongst the stones at the waters edge – along with mussels.

Machynys
'Bass Pool',
Crofty

97

'Slags' (extreme caution required)
NGR 517/964 (Bass Venue)

Bait	Lug, Crab

Low Tide Venue

Walk towards the channel guidance post at Machynys/Llanelli side of the Estuary, a distance of about 1 mile from car park, 4 hours after top water low tide, and as you approach the sea you will see a line of mussel strewn boulders leading out to the post, but there are gaps between the rocks where the tide rushes through.

Walk to the end of the rocks and fish into the Bass holding pools in the river mouth between Machynys Point and Slags Point.

Use a long flowing trace up to 7 feet long, with crab being the top bait.

But be careful if you fish off the rocks, place a marker at low water, and leave after one hour on the incoming tide, otherwise you will be cut off as the tide flows through the gaps in the rocks.

But if you fish off the sand to the left of the stones *(but not so popular)* you can fish the incoming tide longer, with your escape route clear back up to Salthouse Point.

Further round to your left is where you emerge to fish Wernffrwd.

If you take a small rake, you can gather some cockles at the edge of the gullies where the sea runs through the gaps in the rocks, they are just under the sand surface.

Another view of
the 'Bass Pool'

Directions

It is a continuation of fishing the 'Slipway' page 95, but after parking at the roundabout walk at the back of the small cockle processing factory (the side where all the empty cockleshells are stored) through the opening with the steel swing arm gate, across the field, through the gap in the hedge and down the bank. Walk out onto the marsh passing an outfall pipe on your left, then crossing the Salthouse Pill at Crofty.

Another way out to the 'Slags', is by Land Rover. After you pass the Crofty Inn public house, turn right before the small road bridge, and drive down the cockle strewn road passing the area of Holy Thorne, where the Morlais river runs into Salthouse Pill, at Salthouse Point.

Machynys side guidance pole – Penclawdd side pole fallen

Daltons Point

NGR 536/959

Bait	Lugworm, Ragworm

Walk out across the marsh grass crossing some small Pills/Reens, walking slightly to the right for some 300 yards, and fish off the bank approximately $1\frac{1}{2}$ hours either side of top water at the mouth of the gully, in line with the last house and slightly before the playing fields at your back. In front of you across the estuary is the red building of Trostre tinplate works.

NB. This is a low tide venue something in the region of 10.6 metres on the Swansea tide table, because it will flood the pills and cover the marsh grass on a high tide. So check out the area before fishing this venue.

Small amount of harbour ragworm can be dug in the pills, and lugworm along the shoreline before the estuary mouth. Mainly a Flounder venue, but also School Bass.

Comfortable fishing two rods, one long range, one close. Paternoster rig close, Running Ledger type long range.

From the playground at Penclawdd out to Daltons Point

Directions

Come off at junction 47 on the M4, follow the Swansea sign A483 down to the roundabout, turn right signposted A484 to Llanelli, until you see the sign for Gowerton, turn left onto the B4296, travel under the railway bridge, up the hill. Get into the outside lane to turn right at the traffic lights Gower/Llanridian B4295, straight on past mini roundabout, through the traffic lights down to Penclawdd. Just as you leave Penclawdd, at the new housing development of 'Green Acre' (site of old school), and opposite are small boats moored at the area of Daltons Point, drive on some 800 yards and park in small car park on the right hand side, with the marsh grass in front of you.

Two views of the 'Creek' at Daltons Point

Penclawdd Pill/Bacas Sands Area
caution is required all along this stretch of coastline
NGR 546/949

Bait	Ragworm

NGR546/949 – starting point for the walk out on to the marsh.

Arrive at bottom water, or sooner, and after parking the car, walk down the small concrete slipway to cross the first pill which is about the widest and deepest to cross. Problem coming back over this pill unless you wait some $2^1/_2$ hours after top water, you can cross sooner with thigh waders or walk upstream until you can cross.

The walk out over the marsh is about one mile, crossing muddy gullies, head for the Trostre works cooling tower in front of you across the estuary.

Try to arrive out at Bacas sands before the tide has started to make, look for the gullies that the Flounder will swim up at top water.
NB. This is a low tide venue 10.6 to 10.9 metres on the Swansea tide table. The marsh does get flooded on a spring tide.

There are some lugworm out on Bacas sands but be wary of the tide making behind you.

The tide comes up the estuary over the green banks side first, sweeps around the entrance to Gowerton Pill, and back down towards Penclawdd to meet up with the run from Salthouse Point and the Slipway, to leave an island of sand in the middle.

Not over fished during summer months because of crab being troublesome, but during late October/November/December after first frosts, a quite productive Flounder mark, all the way up to the Loughor bridge. A popular mark for competition anglers.

Directions

Come off at junction 47 on the M4 motorway and follow the Swansea sign A483 down to the roundabout, turn right signposted A484 to Llanelli. Follow this road until you see the sign for Gowerton. Turn left onto the B4296, travel under the railway bridge, up the hill, get into the outside lane to turn right at the traffic lights Gower/ Llanridian B4296. Straight on past a mini roundabout, through the traffic lights down to Penclawdd.

In Penclawdd travel around the Z bend and just after the 'Railway Inn'. public house, park the car near the children's playground.

Penclawdd playground area

Gowerton Pill

NGR 562/975

Bait	No

After parking, walk out over the marsh towards Loughor railway and road bridges, try and keep the main pill on your left until nearly out to the end of the marsh, but it is difficult to have an easy walk out. When you arrive at the estuary fish the area some 200 yards from the outfall pipe, where the tide sweeps around and comes back towards you, but this whole area is a productive Flounder venue.

Harbour ragworm can be dug in the pills on the way out.

Remember this is a low tide venue below 11 metres, Swansea tide table, and keep off the sand bar in the middle of the estuary.

Fish approximately $2^{1}/_{2}$ hours before top water and 2 hours after top water. You will have to stay out this length of time because the pills are flooded behind you.

Gowerton Pill before the start of the tide

Directions

As you drive down towards Penclawdd on the B4295 there is a large house on its own on the right hand side, some access out to the marsh between here and the 'Berthlwyd' public house – now closed.

Opposite the 'Berthlwyd' is a tiny layby, parking for only a couple of, cars, do not drive the car down the lane to the small factories, as the gate is locked at night. So leave the car by the apple tree at the right hand concrete gate pillar, and walk down the lane for access out to the marsh.

Not over fished during the summer months because of crab being troublesome, but during late October/November/December after the first frosts, quite a productive Flounder mark, on the way up to the Loughor Bridge, and quite a popular mark for competitive anglers.

Gowerton Pill – Flounder Gully

Gowerton Pill – The Big

Bait	Ragworm

Fish at the corner point off the bank some 20 feet up at low water, the river will come towards you in the shape of a reverse S then goes to the right around a U bend.

On a 11.5 metre tide you will be able to commence fishing $1^{3}/_{4}$ hours before top water, there will be a bit of a run on this height tide, but a breakaway type lead will cope, or plastic breakaway and light 1 or 2oz lead. Light tackle only required, and best fishing during late October/November/December. Crab less troublesome after the frosts.

Mainly Flounder

Gowerton Pill 'The Big' with Loughor Bridge in the background

Directions

When you travel under the railway bridge at Gowerton, turn right at the traffic lights Gower/Llanridian B4296 and at the next set of traffic lights set the mileometer to zero, travel $^{7}/_{10}$ of a mile then watch for the sign LLWY MAWR Farm, Breaking School.

Difficult parking along this stretch of road, but as yet no double yellow lines.

Walk to the right crossing over a gate, after 200 yards turn left and follow a sheep track until you reach a row of square blocks of stone, cross here over a pill, turn right then walk out to the Gowerton Pill 'The Big'.

'The Big' at bottom water

Loughor Bridge Areas
NGR 562/978

Bait	Ragworm

Walk down towards the water, turn left and go through the tunnel under the railway track, you will see at this time the outlet pipe with a stony area to the right. Try some Flounder fishing at low water – winter months.

Try some summer Mullet fishing amongst the railway bridge supports with bread flake, size 4 or 6 hooks with 5lb line. You will lose some tackle but you must keep to light gear for more chance of success, also try harbour ragworm.

Crab troublesome summer months. To the left of the outfall pipe are the mud flats. Dig ragworm (small) amongst the pills and mud.

The art of spiking is still carried on along this stretch of the estuary, (catching Flounder by means of a spike, whilst holding the Flounder beneath your bare foot).

Loughor Castle, built around 1106 AD

Directions

Come off the M4 motorway at junction 47 and follow the Swansea road sign A483 down to the roundabout, turn right on the A484 towards Llanelli. At the next roundabout follow the sign for Llanelli and Gowerton, straight across the next roundabout, passing Gowerton golf range on your left and passing under a road bridge. Then you will come to a sign Loughor A4801 after which is a curved concrete wall – park on the left at the end of this wall, before the mini roundabout.

Road and rail bridges from Cockleshell Island

New Loughor road bridge, from Swansea side

Loughor Boating Club/Tips/Roman Walls

Bait	Ragworm, Limited Crab

Venue 1 – Loughor Bridge *NGR 562/979*

After parking, walk back up the paved area and down onto the steep sloped bank of sand to fish between the railway and road bridges. Mainly Flounder.

Venue 2 – Loughor Boating Club *NGR568/985*

At the mini roundabout, just before Loughor bridge, turn right and take the slip road towards Loughor Boating Club. Travel down the lane at the rear of the boating club, past the factory and park at the end before the gate.

Walk along the path at the top of the bank to the right for some 300 yards, fishing into a steep gully, best on a low tide something just below 11 metres, because of the fast tidal race in the estuary. Above 11 metres, it becomes difficult to hold bottom, and lots of weed on occasions.

Best Flounder fishing the latter part of the year, and especially after the first frosts.

Venue 3 – Roman Walls *NGR 568/997*

At the mini roundabout turn right onto the B4620, drive along to the second mini roundabout and turn left along the B4240 towards Gorseinon. After passing three bollards in the centre of the road turn left past the 'REVEREND JAMES' public house, and down BWLCH road, follow the signs to foreshore car park (the area known as Broad Oak, after the long gone colliery). Park on the right hand side.

Walk to the right along the grass bank to the end, then down the sand bank and across the gully. This gully will fill as the tide comes in, so cross here in plenty of time, (fishing is good along this stretch during winter). Walk along the shoreline past the remains of an old woodland until you come to the ruins of the 'Roman Walls'.

Some crab can be collected at the right time of the year in amongst the stones below the wall, and even ragworm further back at the pills.

Directions

Come off the M4 motorway at junction 47, follow the Swansea road sign A483 down to the roundabout, turn right on the A484 towards Llanelli. At the next roundabout follow the sign for Llanelli and Gowerton, straight across the next roundabout, passing Gowerton golf range on your left, passing under a road bridge, drive up to a mini roundabout. Just before the new Loughor road bridge, turn right, then drive down the slip road on the left to Loughor Boating Club and park at the bottom of the hill to fish beneath Loughor bridge.

Site of old road bridge, Loughor Boating Club in background

Loughor platform to boating club

Cockleshell Island, Loughor

NGR 558/981

Bait	Crab

Just after you cross the new road bridge coming from the Swansea area, there is a small layby on the left hand side before the roundabout, park here and cross the railway track.

Fish to the right hand side of the electrical pylon with tide coming towards you up the estuary. Fishing off a bank of stones, casting onto mud/sand. There are a lot of stones to the left of the pylon. Also worth a try further round to the left along the sand bar gully.

Flounder the main species along this stretch of coastline, best on a low tide something like 10.6 to 10.8 metres.

Crab can be collected amongst the stones at bottom water.

'Cockleshell Island', Loughor

Practice rescue – Loughor Inshore Lifeboat

INA Bearings, Loughor

NGR 560/981

Bait	No

After crossing the new Loughor road bridge, (the original Loughor Bridge was opened on Friday, 7th June, 1834), turn right at the roundabout towards BYNEA on the B4297, then take the first right at the dead end sign, follow the road down to *INA Bearings* car park. At the right hand side, just before the entrance, is a lane going to the right to the bridge, drive down and park at the end of the road.

Flounder fishing all along the sand/mud estuary.

Excellent place to start the youngsters fishing along this stretch, safe and easy, and a good chance for them to catch a fish later in the year.

Try, some Mullet fishing in summer months, at bottom water underneath the railway bridge. Float fishing into the pools using small harbour ragworm, with a light river rod, and small fixed spool reel loaded with 5lb breaking strain line, tiny barrel swivel, some split shot or similar, float, with size 4 or 6 hook. Easy to remember 4-5-6 hook-line-hook.

Alternatively, fish off the road bridge at top water, with a six hook, 6 to 8 foot trace paternoster style for feeding depths (Mullet) with about 8lb breaking strain line and sufficient lead just to hold bottom straight down, also take a long drop net. Try at dusk under the street lights.

Try the following baits: small Ragworm, Bread Flake or the brown tail section of a Whelk before it is cooked.

Loughor Boating Club from INA Bearings. Wreck of a coal barge

Directions – Green Banks, Loughor

Come off the M4 motorway at junction 47, follow the Swansea road sign A483 down to the roundabout, turn right on the A484 towards Llanelli. At the next roundabout follow the signs for Llanelli and Gowerton, straight across the next roundabout passing the Gowerton Golf Range on your left, passing under a road bridge up to a mini roundabout. Turn left across the road bridge, straight on past the next roundabout, and 200 yards past the parking sign is a small layby, to park off the main road.

Go over the stile and across the railway track and walk straight out to the estuary, crossing the main pill by way of a large outfall pipe.

Construction of a new sewerage treatment and pipeworks – progressing September 1997.

Best time of the year fishing the green banks is October to January. Mainly Flounder with some Bass, Mullet and Eels.

Some crab can be collected along the foreshore, amongst the stones, and also under the mud/clay boulders. Easier fishing on a low tide, able to hold bottom. Fast tide race up the estuary.

Green Banks – Remains of old forest, destroyed by tidal wave, 20th January, 1607 at 9 a.m.

Tŷ Coch – Red House

NGR 562/999

Bait	Some Ragworm

After parking, walk across the railway track, taking care especially if you have any youngsters with you.

At the time of writing – straight in front of you and down to the right is a deep gully, but the best fishing at Tŷ Coch is to the left, about 500 yards, where the bank slopes to the water, with the 'Roman Walls' on the opposite side of the, river

This is a Neap tide venue, with fishing best about 10.9 metres down, and around a couple of hours either side of top water, commencing early October through until the end of January, when the crab are less troublesome.

It is an easy venue, and if fishing in inclement weather, take a fishing umbrella, with a small bank offering some protection from the wind. The railway track is just behind you at this point.

Flounder is the main species along this stretch of muddy estuary, try two rods with harbour ragworm obtainable by the Loughor Boating Club, with anti tangle paternoster type rigs.

Heading across the Bay to Tŷ Coch

Directions

Travelling from the Carmarthen and Severn Bridge areas, come off at junction 47 and follow the Swansea A484 sign down to the roundabout, turn right on the A484 and follow this road towards Llanelli. After crossing the Loughor road bridge turn right at the roundabout towards LLWYN HENDY B4297, go over the brow of a small hill with the railway line below, then turn sharp right travelling down Station Road. Carry on until you come round a bend and see three houses facing you, turn right at this point down PENCOED ISAF ROAD, down a narrow lane to the railway track.

Very limited parking because of the narrow lane, please do not cause an obstruction because of careless parking.

Tŷ Coch

Llangennech

Bait	Harbour Ragworm

Your are now fishing the upper reaches of the Loughor Estuary, with a number of nice venues along grassy banks. The tide comes towards you if you are fishing the bank facing Loughor Bridge in the distance. There is a good bend to your right which produces some nice Flounder later on in the year.

If you walk to the end of the narrow road you will come to an outfall pipe and approximately 200 yards past this point is a nice sandy beach where the river runs away from you. As a guide to fishing this venue on a 10.6 metre tide with top water at 13.40p.m., the tide started to make by the outfall pipe at 12.45 and stopped making at 14.10p.m., some 30 minutes longer coming up the estuary. Roughly fish this venue for some $3\frac{1}{2}$ hours with the best tides around 11 metres.

Fishing the Pylon area – the railway police are not too happy about Fishermen walking along the railway track, so walk down the lane on the right hand side in HEOL Y PARC road, follow this down to the foreshore, then cross the railway track and walk along the bank to fish alongside the electrical pylon.

Harbour ragworm is on the decline in the muddy banks. Fishing in the summer months – the crab are a nuisance robbing the bait.

Flounder, Bass, Mullet & Eels.

Llangennech gully at bottom water

Directions

Travelling along the M4 motorway from the Severn Bridge area towards Carmarthen, come off at junction 48, the B4138 Llanelli road, turn left onto the B4297 into Llangennech. Then take the first left after the Co-op food store into Station Road and follow the road down to park on the right hand side by the playing field, before the railway crossing.

Another way to Llangennech from the Swansea area is to come off the M4 at junction 47 and follow the signs to Llanelli A484 and after crossing the Loughor Bridge turn right at the roundabout towards LLWYN HENDY B4297. Over the brow of a small hill, turn right into Station Road. Drive for just over one mile to the T-junction by the Royal Oak public house on your left. Turn right just before the garage into HEOL Y PARC road and so on to the playing field.

Outfall pipe at Llangennech – sandy beach 200 yards to the left

Holiday Camp Sites

If you intend bringing a touring caravan, trailer tent or tent to the Peninsula, I have put together the sites available, complete with my own photographs, and not the brochure photographs which are possibly misleading.

I have used the national grid reference numbers for ease of location, and distance from beach etc.

It is worth just booking a couple of nights, if it is your first visit, and to travel around Gower to see the site most suitable for you and your family.

Bank Farm, Horton
Gower, Swansea. SA3 1LL
Telephone No.: 01792 390228
NGR 469/859

Carreglwyd
Site Office, Port Eynon
Gower, Swansea. SA3 1NN
Telephone No.: 01792 390795
NGR 467/850

Greenways Holiday Park
Oxwich Bay
Gower, Swansea. SA3 1LY
Telephone No.: 01792 390220/
01792 390291

Tents and Trailer Tents only.
Luxury Bungalows and
Luxury Caravans to let.
NGR 495/864

Newpark Holiday Park
Port Eynon
Gower, Swansea. SA3 1NP
Telephone No.: 01792 390292

Oxwich Camping Park
Oxwich, Gower
Swansea. SA3 1LS
Telephone No.: 01792 390777

Tent and Motorhomes only
NO PETS
NGR 496/868

Port Eynon Youth Hostel
Port Eynon (on sea shore)
Telephone Number: 01792 390706

Oxwich Bay Hotel
Gower, Swansea. SA3 1LS
Telephone Number: 01792 390329
NGR 502/863

Siting at the Oxwich Bay Hotel is
for the full season only, at a cost
for 1998 of £1000 plus V.A.T.
Only six plots within the site.
Waiting list – no sites available

Gowerton Caravan Club Site
Pont-y-Cob Road
Gowerton, Swansea. SA4 3QP
Telephone Number: 01792 873050
NGR 581/969

Pitton Cross Caravan Park
Rhossili, Gower, Swansea. SA3 1PH
Telephone Number: 01792 390593
NGR 435/877

Clyne Farm and Activity Centre
Telephone Number: 01792 403333

Swansea Bay Tourism Office
Telephone Number: 01792 403339

Sea Weeds

Prior to eating, as our sea water is not always in pristine condition, soak in fresh clean tap water with a small quantity of the dark crystals of POTASSIUM PERMANGANATE for half an hour, then thoroughly wash out in cold water, the crystals will remove all the unsavoury aquatic organisms. The crystals can be obtained from the chemists in a small container. Just a small quantity required to turn the water purple.

Laverweed (Laverbread) – "Porphyra Umbilicalis"

Sea Laver is picked off the rocks towards bottom water, it is the black seaweed stuck flat to the rocks, you can feel it peeling off the stones when collecting.

To Prepare: Thoroughly clean, using the crystals and finish off by running under the cold tap. With the weed in a colander cut up small with a scissors, and cook in small batches, unless you have a large cooking utensil. (*NB: Take care if you try and mince in a food processor, it tends to burn out the motor, so be warned – I know!*)

Cooking: Rub the inside of a large saucepan with margarine, place in the Laver with a small quantity of water and bring to the boil, turn down the heat and simmer. Add more hot water when required to stop the weed and saucepan burning. After about one hour start adding slowly the seasoning, Pepper and Vinegar and very – very careful with the salt. Continue simmering for about another two hours adding seasoning to your taste. But remember to watch that the Laverbread does not stick to the pan and burn. It will finally turn to a thick paste like substance.

Samphire

The Sea Asparagus, two types: Marsh and Rock.

To prepare Marsh Samphire: Use the crystals to clean and remove any sand/grit particles. Cut off the rough part of the stem. Blanch quickly in hot water to remove some of the salty taste, then fry lightly in olive oil butter, but experiment.

When collecting cut with a scissors or shears just above the sand/ mud to leave the roots intact.

Shell Fish, Eel & Shrimp

Crab

After collecting bring the Crab home alive by wrapping them individually in a damp saltwater cloth, then place in your bag or rucksack. Please only bring a couple of the larger ones home.

Cooking: No Condiments, season to taste after. Bring a large saucepan of water to the boil, and just before immersing the Crab into the boiling water, for humane reasons kill the Crab by lifting the tail flap and inserting the point of a clean baiting needle or skewer into the body. The cooking time for any size Crab is 20 to 25 Minutes, let the Crab cool naturally, then break off the claws cracking them open with a 'Toffee Hammer' taking care when extracting the white meat that all the shell is removed. Prise the top shell from the body, discard the two sets of five finger grey gills *(Dead Man's Fingers)* and the small stomach sac, which is usually left behind in the top shell behind the eyes. All the rest is edible. No poisonous parts in the Crab, but the Grey Gills are unedible – they taste horrible!

When you get to this stage, practice, patience and experience will determine how much white Crab meat can be extracted with a skewer or better still, with wooden barbecue kebab skewers from the claws and the honeycomb body section.

Mix some bread crumbs with a selection of herbs of your choice, Chives, Onions, Shallots, Garlic etc. Into this mixture place the soft brown Crab meat, mix together and place to one side of the cleaned top Crab shell, place the white Crab meat on the other side and cover with cling film.

Crab meat freezes well.

Cockles

Collecting: Cockles are found just below the sand surface, to collect, you need a small hand rake, sieve, and a onion type sack. I wear chest waders so I can kneel down to rake them up, be careful not to tear them on the shells.

The minimum size are between 17.5 mm to 19 mm, approximately 3/4 of an inch. *(See my gauge drawing - page 137).*

When you find a Cockle bed kneel down and use the rake to

remove the Cockles from the sand into a pile and place the Cockles & mud/sand into the sieve, you will usually find a pool of sea water to riddle the Cockles clean. There is a legal limit on the amount you can take, so just take enough to cook in one session.

Cooking: When you get the Cockles home, tip them into a bucket and with the garden hose pipe wash the Cockles stirring continuously with your hands, until the water comes back to clean. Into a large saucepan place some tap water, *(without salt)* tip in a couple of handfuls of the Cockles so that the water is just covering them, bring to the boil and as soon as the water comes up to the boil and the Cockle shells open, they are cooked. Tip them into a colander and run under a cold tap until cool, then separate the Cockles from the shell.

Now comes the best part, the Cockles are full of the black gritty muck that all the books say before cooking, soak overnight in salt or Porridge Oats! to clean before cooking.

My Recipe: Use your clean hands to squeeze the Cockles whilst running under the cold tap with them still in the colander, keep squeezing lightly until they are completely free of grit and clean. Not an ounce of salt used from collecting to the plate, completely fresh. Now you can season to taste.

You can tell the age of a Cockle by the number of rings on the shell. Two the first year, then one every other year.

Some types of Cockle: QUEENS, STUKY BLUES and the juvenile known as SPATS. The name of the common Cockle is CARDRUM EDULE.

MUSSELS

Can be found on the rocks over a large area of Gower, do not be surprised when you find small Red Striped Crabs living happily inside some of the larger Mussels.

You have seen Mussels being cooked on television then being eaten straight out of the shell. I would suggest a word of caution here, the difference between Farmed and Wild Mussels. The Farmed have been scrubbed clean .The hair that grips the wild Mussel to the rocks *(The Byssus)* goes through the shell and into the Mussels body, which should be removed after cooking – unmistakable.

Wash the Mussels clean in a bucket of cold water.

Cooking: In a large saucepan just cover the shells with cold water *(no salt)* and bring to the boil, the shells will have opened and the Mussel will be cooked. If the shell is still closed or damaged – discard. Run under the cold tap in a colander and remove the Mussel from the shell, check every one and remove the BYSSUS hair. Leave to rest in the fridge with herbs and condiments of your choice.

Winkles

Thoroughly wash the Winkles in a sieve, place the shells in a saucepan and just cover with water *(no salt)* and bring to the boil, turn down the heat and just simmer for about five minutes, the longer you leave them cooking the tougher they become.

Extract the snail from the shell with a pin or similar implement, then cut off the snails brown 'DOOR' with a scissors. Place the shelled snails in a bowl and sprinkle with Pepper and Vinegar.

Small Conger Eel

Try cooking by cutting the Eel into cutlet type pieces, and skin them separately, or simply bar boil to loosen the skin. Bake or fry.

The thick end of the EEL is best, the tail section is very bony.

Shrimps

Do not linger after collecting your Shrimps, because they need to be cooked as soon as possible, keep cool with freezer packs in your container whilst returning home.

Boil the Shrimps for about two to three minutes, they will float to the surface and are cooked *(no salt)*. Allow to cool, peel, chill in the fridge, or eat straight away.

Not a good freezer.

2 Hook Crab Beater

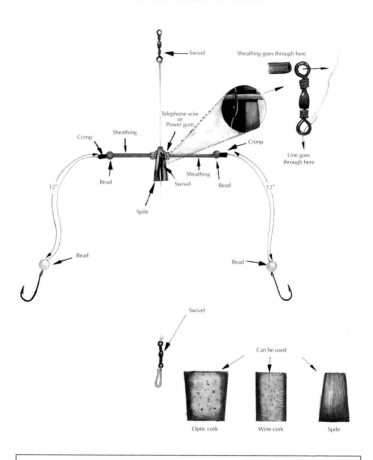

Materials used

5" Electrical Sheathing

3 Swivels – 2 x size 6
          1 x size 8

Telephone wire or
   power gum

2 Crimps

4 Beads – 2 of 5mm
         2 of 8mm

50lb Shock Leader

20lb Amnesia Snood

1 Genie Linkclip

2 Hooks

Clipped Pulley

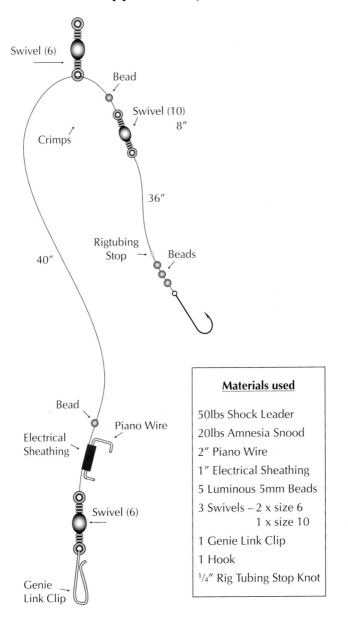

Swivel (6)

Bead

Swivel (10)
8"

Crimps

36"

Rigtubing
Stop → Beads

40"

Bead
Piano Wire
Electrical
Sheathing

Swivel (6)

Genie
Link Clip

Materials used

50lbs Shock Leader
20lbs Amnesia Snood
2" Piano Wire
1" Electrical Sheathing
5 Luminous 5mm Beads
3 Swivels – 2 x size 6
1 x size 10
1 Genie Link Clip
1 Hook
1/4" Rig Tubing Stop Knot

Rotten Bottom

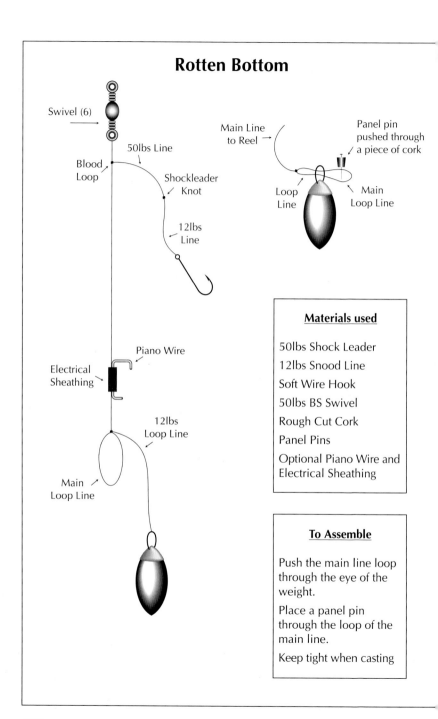

Swivel (6)

50lbs Line

Blood Loop

Shockleader Knot

12lbs Line

Main Line to Reel

Panel pin pushed through a piece of cork

Loop Line

Main Loop Line

Piano Wire

Electrical Sheathing

12lbs Loop Line

Main Loop Line

Materials used

50lbs Shock Leader

12lbs Snood Line

Soft Wire Hook

50lbs BS Swivel

Rough Cut Cork

Panel Pins

Optional Piano Wire and Electrical Sheathing

To Assemble

Push the main line loop through the eye of the weight.

Place a panel pin through the loop of the main line.

Keep tight when casting

Clipped Lead Beach Bomb

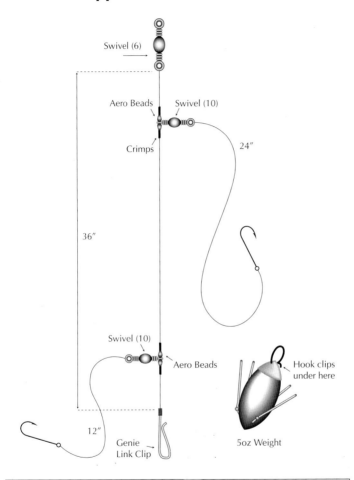

Swivel (6)

Aero Beads   Swivel (10)

Crimps   24″

36″

Swivel (10)

Aero Beads

Hook clips
under here

12″

Genie
Link Clip

5oz Weight

Materials used

3 Swivels – 1 x size 6, 2 x size 10   2 Hooks
1 Genie Link Clip   50lbs Shock Leader
4 Crimps   20lbs Amnesia Snood
4Aero Beads   5oz Clipped Lead

Clipped Pennell

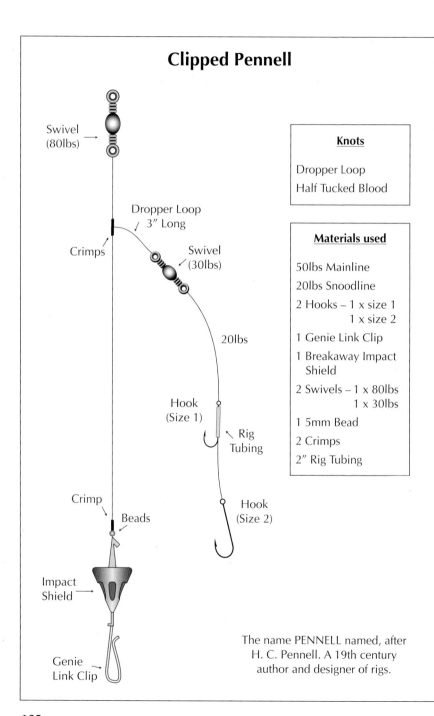

Swivel (80lbs)

Dropper Loop
3" Long

Crimps

Swivel
(30lbs)

20lbs

Hook
(Size 1)

Rig
Tubing

Hook
(Size 2)

Crimp

Beads

Impact
Shield

Genie
Link Clip

Knots

Dropper Loop
Half Tucked Blood

Materials used

50lbs Mainline
20lbs Snoodline
2 Hooks – 1 x size 1
          1 x size 2
1 Genie Link Clip
1 Breakaway Impact
  Shield
2 Swivels – 1 x 80lbs
          1 x 30lbs
1 5mm Bead
2 Crimps
2" Rig Tubing

The name PENNELL named, after
H. C. Pennell. A 19th century
author and designer of rigs.

Flounder Rig
One hook below, one hook above

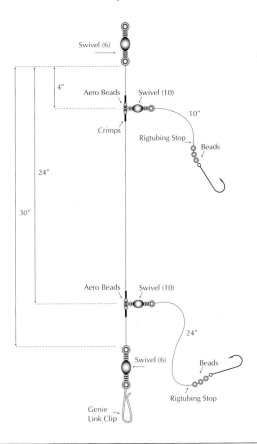

Swivel (6)

4″

Aero Beads   Swivel (10)

10″

Crimps

Rigtubing Stop

Beads

24″

30″

Aero Beads   Swivel (10)

24″

Swivel (6)

Beads

Rigtubing Stop

Genie Link Clip

Materials used

4 Swivels –
  (2 x size 6, 2 x size 8)
1 Genie Link Clip
4 Crimps
4Aero Beads

2 Hooks
50lbs Shock Leader
20lbs Amnesia Snood
6 x 8mm Beads
$1/4$″ Rig Tubing Stop

3 Hook Running Paternoster

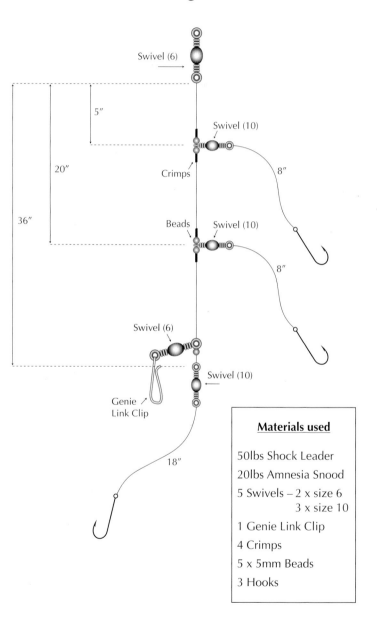

Swivel (6)

5"

Swivel (10)

20"

Crimps

8"

36"

Beads   Swivel (10)

8"

Swivel (6)

Swivel (10)

Genie
Link Clip

18"

Materials used

50lbs Shock Leader

20lbs Amnesia Snood

5 Swivels – 2 x size 6
              3 x size 10

1 Genie Link Clip

4 Crimps

5 x 5mm Beads

3 Hooks

Flounder Rig Hooks Above

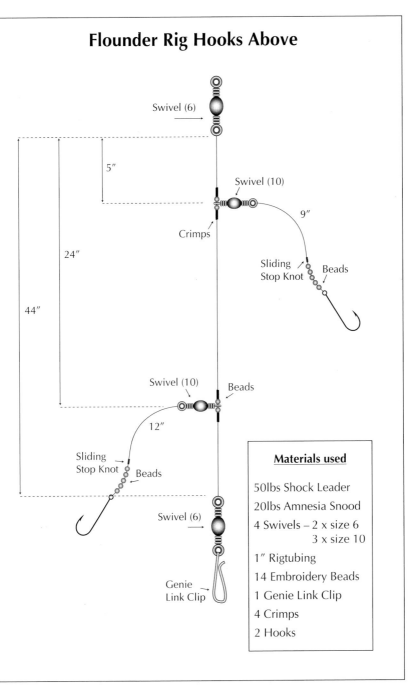

Swivel (6)

5″

Swivel (10)

9″

Crimps

24″

Sliding
Stop Knot

Beads

44″

Swivel (10)

Beads

12″

Sliding
Stop Knot

Beads

Swivel (6)

Genie
Link Clip

Materials used

50lbs Shock Leader

20lbs Amnesia Snood

4 Swivels – 2 x size 6
3 x size 10

1″ Rigtubing

14 Embroidery Beads

1 Genie Link Clip

4 Crimps

2 Hooks

135

Lobster and Crab Gauge Guide

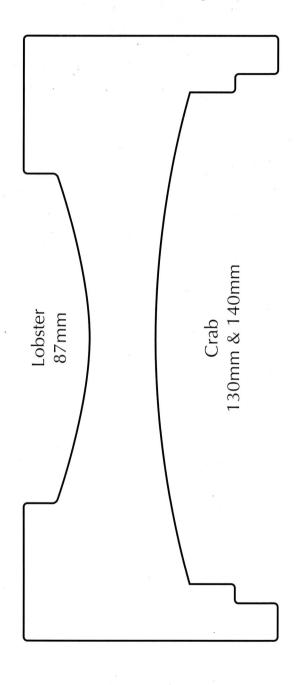

Lobster
87 mm

Crab
130mm & 140mm

Multigauge
~ *Oyster, Cockle, Mussel, Winkle* ~

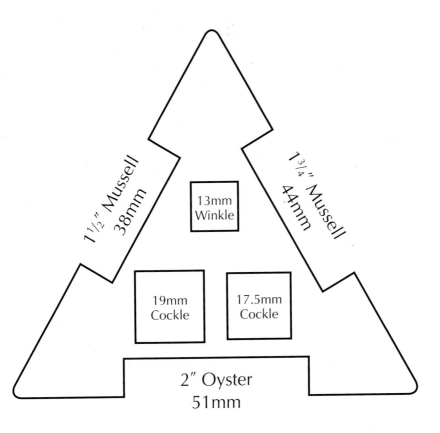

You can make templates off these gauges if it will help to preserve our stocks

ASSOCIATED BRITISH PORTS
SOUTH WALES PORTS

In consideration of your permitting.. to fish from

SWANSEA   :   The West Pier only

PORT TALBOT :   Former South & Stone Piers

NB: Please tick which location applies

I hereby agree (to the fullest extent permitted by law) to be responsible for and to release and indemnify ABP it's servants and agents from and against all liability for:-

(a)   Personal injury (whether fatal or otherwise) save to the extent that Section 2(1) of the Unfair Contract Terms Act 1977 shall be applicable.

(b)   Loss of or damage to any property whatsoever, and

(c)   and other loss (including economic loss) damage, costs and expenses howsoever caused or incurred (whether or not caused or contributed to by the negligent act or default of ABP, it's servants or agent arising directly or indirectly from or in any way connected with the above mentioned permission.

I do further undertake and agree in the event of this permission being renewed by ABP at any time or times, and in every case this Agreement shall be considered as a continuing one, and shall extend and apply to any and every renewal in the same manner and with the like effect as if the Agreement were expressly entered in upon each and every renewal.

Dated this...................................day of..

Name   ....

Signature ....

Address   ....

          ....

Witness to the above:

Name   ....

Signature..

Address ....

          ....

In the event of the applicant being aged 16 to 18 years of age, the Indemnity should be signed by a Parent or Guardian.
In consideration of your allowing the above named person to enter upon your premises I undertake and declar that as long as he/she is under 18 years of age, I will well and effectually indemnify you against all loss or liab of any kind whatsoever which may be sustained or incurred by you by reason of or in consequence of his meeting with any injury or accident while upon your premises.

I acknowledge that the above mentioned permission may be withdrawn by ABP at any time.

138

Minimum Fish Sizes

The minimum size limits prescribed for sea fish in this district are set out below – in centimetres:

Bass	37.5cm
Blue Ling	70.0cm
Cod	35.0cm
Grey Mullet	35.0cm
Haddock	30.0cm
Hake	27.0cm
Herring	20.0cm
Horse Mackerel (Scad)	15.0cm
Ling	63.0cm
Mackerel	20.0cm
Megrim	25.0cm
Plaice	27.0cm
Pollack	30.0cm
Red Mullet	15.0cm
Saithe	35.0cm
Skate and Ray	45.0cm	*Across wings*
" " "	22.0cm	*Single detached wing*
Sole	24.0cm
Whiting	27.0cm
Lobster	9.0cm	*Carapace length (max size pending)*
Nephrops	8.5cm	*Overall length (ICES VIIa 7.0cm)*
	4.6cm	*Tails (ICES VIIa 3.7cm)*
Edible Crab	14.0cm	*Across broad of back*
Velvet Crab	6.5cm	*Across broad of back, excluding spines*
Crawfish	11.0cm	*Carapace length*
Spider Crab	12.0cm	*Carapace length*
Scallop	11.0cm	*Across broad part of the flat shell*
Queen Scallop (Chlamys spp)	4.0cm
Grooved Carpetshell (Ruditapes decussatus)	4.0cm -
Carpetshell (Venerupis pullastra)	3.8cm
Short-necked Clam (Ruditapes philippinarum)	4.0cm
Clam (Venus verucosa)	4.0cm
Hard Clam (Callista chione)	6.0cm
Razor Clam (Ensis siliqua)	10.0cm
Surf Clam (Spisula solidissima)	2.5cm
Donax Clams (Donax spp)	2.5cm
Bean Solen (Pharus legumen)	6.5cm

South Wales Sea Fisheries Commitee

Queens Buildings
Cambrian Place
Swansea. SA1 1TW

Tel: 01792 654466
Fax: 01792 645987
E.mail: SWSFC@aol.com

Periwinkle – Must not pass through square aperture of 13mm (0.5″)
Oyster – Must not pass through circular aperture of 51mm (2″) diameter
Cockle – Must not pass through square aperture of 19mm (¾″) – *unless by authorisation*
Mussel – In length 51mm (2″) – *unless by authorisation*
Whelk – Must not pass through square aperture of 35mm (1.38″) – *25mm by authorisation*

One to remember

Welsh National Anthem

Mae hen wlad fy Nhadau, yn annwyl i mi,
Gwlad beirdd a chantorion enwogion o fri;
Ei gwrol ryfelwyr, gwladgarwyr tra mad,
Dros ryddid collasant eu gwaed.
Gwlad, Gwlad, pleidiol wyf i'm gwlad;
Tra mor yn fur i'r bur hoff bau
O bydded i'r hen iaith barhau.

The old land of my fathers is dear to me,
Land of poets and singers, famous men of renown;
Its brave warriors, fine patriots,
Gave their blood for freedom.
My country, My country, I am devoted to my country,
While the sea is a wall to the pure loved land
O may the old language endure.

Written by EVAN JAMES of Pontypridd, his son composed the music.
First published in 1860. English words by DYFED WYN EDWARDS.

Conclusion

Within the Gower Peninsula – which is only approximately 16 miles long by 4 to 7 miles wide – we have some of the best scenery in the British Isles. To name just a few: the Worms Head, Llangennith, the ornithologists bird station after the Hooper Banks tope channel...

The book concentrates mainly on fishing from the beaches and rock venues. But for the boat angler, Turbot bank at Slade; Tope and Conger at Pwlldu; Bream and Bass at Langland; Cod, Tope and Conger out from Caswell to Westminster; Mackerel at Mixon to Bass at Paviland reef, plus many more marks.

We as anglers have the monopoly of our beautiful coastline for eight to nine months of the year, so can we leave them in pristine condition, not with discarded bait bags, and other rubbish, so that our Summer visitors can learn from our example.

On our Bass fishing, can we carry out a catch and release policy, enjoy our sport. Hopefully the 40cm size limit will be in shortly.

Do not forget to buy the Swansea tide table booklet, there are some caution venues to watch out for.

Finally, every effort has been made in the writing of this book to be as accurate as possible, but there will be some changes, for which I apologise.

– GOOD LUCK –
GOD BLESS & BEST WISHES

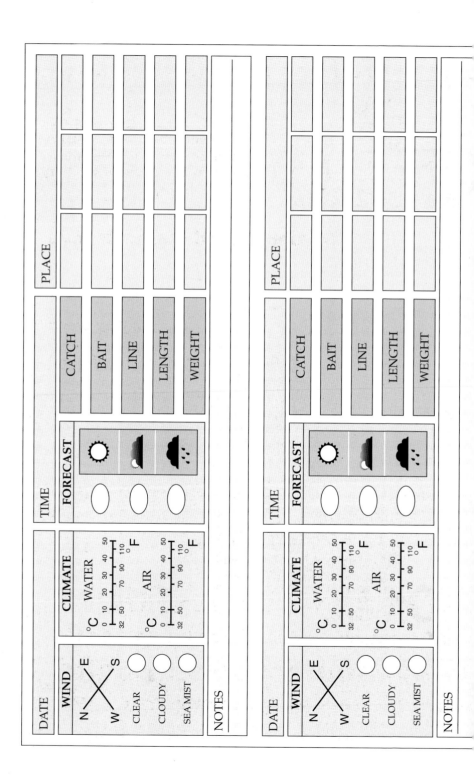

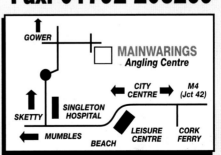